HÄDECKE

Original Fränkisch
The Best of Franconian Food

Abkürzungen und Maße

Pck – Päckchen
Ø – Durchmesser
cm – Zentimeter
g – Gramm
kg – Kilogramm
ml – Milliliter = 0,001 Liter
l – Liter
TL – Teelöffel
EL – Esslöffel

Beim Löffelmaß handelt es sich immer um das gestrichene Maß.

Die Rezepte sind, soweit nicht anders vermerkt, für 4 Portionen.

Abbreviations and measurements

lb – pound(s)
oz – ounce(s)
tbsp – tabelspoon(s)
tsp – teaspoon(s)
1 pint (Amer.) is approx. 1/2 liter.
1 tbsp is about 1/2 fl oz.
1 tsp is about 1/5 fl oz.
1 pinch is about 1/8 teaspoon.

All teaspoon and tablespoon measurement are level spoons.

If not otherwise indicated, the recipes yield 4 servings.

HÄDECKE

Franziska Hanel

Orginal Fränkisch The Best of Franconian Food

Fotos von
Angela Francisca Endress

Rezepte

Recipes

1

2

3

7

8

10

11

12

4

5

6

9

Fränkische Impressionen
Impressions of Franconia

13

14

Frankens kulinarische Vielfalt

Aus Würzburg kommt das älteste Kochbuch in deutscher Sprache, das „*Buoch von guoter spîse*". Handschriftlich, auf feinem Pergament notiert, waren es rund fünfzig Rezepte, die eine Ahnung davon vermitteln, was im Mittelalter gegessen wurde. Michael de Leone hat die interessante Sammlung im Jahr 1340 angelegt. Der fürstbischöfliche Verwaltungsbeamte nannte sich nach seinem Hof zum Löwen zu Würzburg.

Von dieser Handschrift abzuleiten, dass man im schönen Frankenland kulinarischen Genüssen früher zugeneigt war als in anderen deutschen Regionen, ist vielleicht Spekulation. Tatsache ist aber, dass man es im kunstfertigen, weltaufgeschlossenen Franken seit jeher verstand, fürstlich zu tafeln – den Bischofssitzen, Ritterburgen, Schlössern und Patriziern sei Dank. Und natürlich färbte die Kunst zu speisen auf die Bürger und Bauern ab.

Man hatte Vieles, was zu einem guten Essen gehört, direkt vor der Haustür – das ist auch noch heute so. Und die Besonderheiten der vielfältigen Landschaften Frankens finden sich auf den Tellern wieder.

Zum Beispiel Gemüse in Hülle und Fülle. Wie vom Gemüseanbaugebiet nördlich von Nürnberg, das sich als „*Knoblauchsland*" einen Namen gemacht hat, wie von den Bamberger Gärtnern, die als „*Zwiebeltreter*" in die Geschichte eingegangen sind. Darunter Meerrettich (auch in Franken Kren genannt), der viele typische Gerichte mit pikanter Schärfe aufpeppt. Dazu Salate und Kohlsorten aller Art, Gurken, Möhren, Kürbis, Kartoffeln, die urkundlich belegt seit dem 17. Jahrhundert angebaut werden – heute auch Tomaten, Auberginen und andere Vertreter mediterraner Gemüsesorten, die in Gewächshäusern reifen. Oder der fränkische Spargel, der sich in Unterfranken rund um Volkach und in Mittelfranken von Erlangen bis Gunzenhausen angesiedelt hat und zum lukullischen Dauerbrenner im Frühling geworden ist. Nicht nur klassisch mit Schinken, neuen Kartöffelchen und holländischer Soße entzückt er den Gaumen der Feinschmecker, sondern ebenso in profaner, wenngleich unwiderstehlicher Kombination mit Bratwürsten. Dazu ein Glas Frankenwein, und man fühlt sich dem Himmel auf Erden schon näher.

Ja, auch Wein wächst in Franken. Und das schon ziemlich lange. Im Mittelalter war Franken innerhalb des Heiligen Römischen Reichs das größte Weinanbaugebiet nördlich der Alpen. Obschon die Fläche seit dieser Zeit geschrumpft ist, prägen nach wie vor Rebstöcke die Region im lieblichen Maindreieck zwischen Spessart, Rhön, Steigerwald sowie Taubertal und die Menschen dort leben vom Weinanbau und Weinverkauf. Längst vergangen sind die Zeiten, als Frankenwein ein Sauerampfer-Image hatte. Viele Winzer produzieren heute Spitzenweine, darunter Riesling, der durch seinen eigenwilligen Charakter überzeugt. Die häufigste Rebsorte ist der Müller-Thurgau mit seinem duftigen und blumigen Bukett. An den steilen Weinbergen im Maindreieck werden Silvaner angebaut, die zu den besten der Welt zählen.

Bezeichnend für Frankenwein ist der bauchige Bocksbeutel. Seit dem frühen 18. Jahrhundert werden in ihn Qualitätsweine abgefüllt. Als Markenzeichen ist die berühmte Flaschenform in der Europäischen Union geschützt. Und sie ist beliebt, bei Weinproben ebenso wie bei den vielen Weinfesten, die Tausende von Weinliebhabern Jahr für Jahr ins fränkische Weinland locken.

Natürlich wird mit Wein auch gekocht. Ein Gläschen verfeinert viele Saucen und Suppen. Mehr davon wird zur feinen Marinade für Fleisch und Geflügel.

Das gilt auch fürs Bier, das vor allem den Oberfranken seinen Stempel aufgedrückt hat. Hervorragendes Wasser und sehr gute Bedingungen für den Anbau von Braugerste machen Oberfranken zur Region mit der größten Brauereidichte der Welt. Dort wurde im späten 18.–19. Jahrhundert auch noch Hopfen angebaut, wofür heute vor allem

Franconia's culinary abundance

The oldest German language cookery book, the "Buoch von guoter spîse", or "book of good meals", comes from Würzburg. The handwritten collection, which was recorded in 1340 by Michael de Leone, contains about fifty recipes written on fine parchment and gives us an inkling of the kind of food eaten in the Middle Ages. De Leone, a prince bishopric's civil servant, took the name of his estate, "The Lion of Würzburg". To conclude that the people living in the beautiful region of Franconia indulged their fondness for good food earlier than those in other regions, purely on the basis of these writings, is perhaps speculation. However, it is a fact that thanks to the episcopal sees, castles, palaces and patricians, the skilled and cosmopolitan people of Franconia had long known how to eat well. And, of course, this art of dining well rubbed off on the local citizens and farmers.

Many of the things you need for a good meal was available right at their doorstep, and the same is true today. The specialities of the diverse Franconian countryside are reflected in the local dishes. The vegetable farming region north of Nuremberg that made its name as "Garlic County", along with the gardeners of Bamberg who have gone down in history as "onion treaders" are both home to a multitude of vegetable dishes. Then there's horseradish (also known in Franconia as "Kren"), which is used to spice up many typical dishes. And you'll find all sorts of lettuces, cabbage varieties, cucumbers, carrots, pumpkins, and potatoes – which are documented as having been cultivated in the region since the 17th century – along with tomatoes, eggplants and other Mediterranean vegetables which ripen in greenhouses these days.

Then there's Franconian asparagus which has become a gourmet hit that's enjoyed every spring. It's cultivated throughout Lower Franconia, in the area around Volkach, and throughout Middle Franconia in a region that stretches from Erlangen to Gunzenhausen. There you'll find it served, not just traditionally with ham, new potatoes and hollandaise sauce, but also in more down to earth but irresistible style – with grilled sausages. All you'll need then is a glass of Franconian wine, and it'll feel like heaven on earth just got a little closer.

And yes, wine is grown in Franconia – and it has been for quite a while. During the Middle Ages, Franconia was the largest wine growing region north of the Alps in the Holy Roman Empire. Even if the wine growing region has shrunk since then, vineyards still characterize the beautiful countryside of the "Maindreieck", which is the area between Spessart, the Rhön, Steigerwald and Taubertal. Long gone are the days when Franconian wine had a reputation for being sour. The locals make a living from wine production and today's wine growers produce top quality wines like Riesling that is highly valued for its unique character. The predominant grape in the region is the Müller-Thurgau, with its flowery, scented bouquet, and some of the world's best Silvaners are produced on the steep slopes of the "Maindreieck". Bocksbeutel wine bottles are synonymous with high quality Franconian wine, and have been in use since the 18th century. The unusually shaped bottle is famous and is protected under EU law. It is popular both at wine tastings, and at the many wine festivals that draw thousands of visitors to Franconia every year.

And of course, local wine is used for cooking. One glass will finish off a sauce or soup perfectly, although a bit more is needed for delicious meat and poultry marinades. The same goes for beer, which has particularly made its mark in Upper Franconia. Excellent water and very good conditions for growing brewer's barley make Upper Franconia the region with the highest concentration of breweries in the world. Hops were also grown here from the late 18th century until the late 19th century, and nowadays Middle Franconia is particularly famous for its hops. There are more breweries here than in any other German federal state or other

Mittelfranken berühmt ist. Es gibt in Oberfranken mehr Brauereien, als jedes Bundesland in Deutschland und jedes Land Europas zu bieten hat. Zur sogenannten fünften Jahreszeit, die in Oberfranken beispielsweise bereits im Oktober beginnt, kann man von Bockbieranstich zu Bockbieranstich lustwandeln. Das ist einer der Höhepunkte der Biersaison, die mit viel Klamauk und Kulinaria verbunden sind. An die tausend verschiedene Biere werden gebraut, und ständig kommen neue, interessante Geschmacksvarianten dazu, erfunden von kreativen jungen Braumeistern und zunehmend auch -meisterinnen. Am besten schmeckt „*a Seidla*" – so nennt man einen halben Liter Bier auf Fränkisch – im Wirtshaus, Biergarten oder auf einem der vielen Volks- und Schützenfeste. Die herzhafte Grundlage dafür kann eine zünftige Brotzeit wie „*Nürnberger Gwerch*" (Seite 14), „*Coburger Zwiebelfleisch*" (Seite 18) oder eine „*Kulmbacher Bierhaxe*" (Seite 50) sein.

Rezepte in Sachen Kartoffel gibt es im Fichtelgebirge und im Frankenwald zuhauf. Sogar leckere Blechkuchen, wie der „*Erpflkoung mit Rosinen*" (Seite 60) aus dem Hofer Land, werden mit „Erdäpfeln" hergestellt. Natürlich auch die Klöße, die auf Fränkisch „Glees" heißen. Ein Bratengericht ist ohne den Kloß als Beilage einfach nicht vollständig. Doch man muss zugeben, dass die Kunst des Klößemachens, egal ob rohe (grüne) oder halbseidene Klöße (baumwollne, mit gekochten Kartoffeln, Seite 56) in Zeiten des fertigen Kloßteigs ein bisschen in Vergessenheit geraten ist. Aber was die Beliebtheit des Kartoffelkloßes betrifft, hat sich nichts geändert – und der „Kloß mit Soß'" wird nicht nur von Kindern heiß geliebt.

Manche Zeitgenossen essen Klöße sogar zu Fisch, wie zu Karpfen. Die wiederum sind eine Spezialität besonders ab Oktober, wenn die Teiche abgefischt werden. Kenner rühmen die Aischgründer Spiegelkarpfen im Zentrum der fränkischen Fischwirtschaft. Doch es gibt überall in der Region kleine Karpfenzüchter, die die Wirtshäuser in der Nachbarschaft bedienen und dafür sorgen, dass in den Monaten mit „*r*" immer frischer Fisch auf den Tisch kommt. Auch Forellen und Saiblinge, Waller, Hecht und anderes Flossengetier sind beliebte Speisen, die am liebsten „blau" oder gebacken zubereitet werden.

So ist das im Land der Franken: Man pflegt sein kulturelles Erbe, probiert aber sehr gerne Neues. Man liebt Pizza, Gyros & Co., weicht aber – „weil es nichts Besseres gibt als was Gutes" – von seinen traditionellen Leibspeisen nicht ab. Was die Großmama kocht, schätzt der Enkel sein Leben lang: Ein knuspriges *Schäufele* (Seite 38) mit Sauerkraut und Klößen, eine zarte Surhaxe mit Stampf (Schweinehaxe mit Kartoffelpüree), ein *Karpfen* mit goldfarbener Kruste (Seite 26), begleitet von köstlichem, *lauwarmen Kartoffelsalat* (Seite 56), ein frisch gebackener *Zwetschgerblootz* (Seite 66) am Sonntag zum Kaffee und vieles mehr lädt ein zu unserer Rezepttour durch Franken.

European country. During the so called fifth season*, which begins in October in Franconia, the breweries celebrate the first tapping of the beer barrels. This forms the highpoint of the beer season, a time when beer lovers can stroll from one event to another, and food and fun are abundant.

Roughly one thousand different beers are brewed by the creative young master beer brewers in the region, with new and interesting flavours constantly being added to the list with the number of young female master brewers on the rise. "a Seidla", the name for a pint of beer in the Franconian dialect, tastes best of all in the taverns, beer gardens or at one of the many "Volksfeste" and "Schützenfeste" (public street festivals and shooting match festivals). The ideal food to eat beforehand can be a snack like "Nuremberg Mess" (page 15), "Coburg Meat and Onion Salad" (page 19) or "Kulmbach Beer Knuckles" (page 51).

When it comes to potatoes there are piles of recipes from the Fichtelgebirge and Frankenwald. There's even a cake recipe from Hofer Land called, "Potato Cake with Raisins" (page 61) that uses potatoes. And of course there are the dumplings, known in Franconia as "Glees". A traditional roast is not complete unless served with a dumpling, but it has to be said that these days, where it's possible to buy ready-made dumpling dough, the art of dumpling making – whether it's the raw (green) dumplings or the silky ones (made with cooked potatoes) – seems to have been forgotten. However, dumplings are still as popular as ever, and it's not just children who really love "Kloß mit Soß" (dumplings with gravy). There are even some people who like to eat dumplings with fish, for example with carp.

These are a speciality from October onwards, when the breeding ponds are emptied. Connoisseurs rave about the mirror carp from Aischgründ, the centre of Franconia's fish farming industry. But there are small carp breeders throughout the region who supply the local taverns and make sure that fresh fish are available during the months where the names of the month in German contain the letter "R", e. g., October through to February. Trout and char, catfish, pike, and other fish are popular dishes, preferably prepared "blue" in wine broth, or baked.

So that's life in Franconia: they maintain their cultural heritage, but like to try new things. People like to eat pizza and gyros and the like, but they don't neglect the old favourites, since their maxim is – "There's nothing better than something that's good!"

Whatever Grandma used to cook is what a people love for life: a crispy pork shoulder (page 39) with sauerkraut and dumplings; a succulent "Surhaxe mit Stampf" (knuckle of pork with mashed potato); baked carp with a golden crust (page 27) accompanied by delicious warm potato salad (page 57); freshly baked damson cake with crumble topping (page 67) for Sunday tea. This and much more is on offer when you take our culinary tour through Franconia.

* Carnival season in Germany (Mardi Gras)

Nürnberger Gwerch
Nuremberg Sausage Salad

Nürnberger Gwerch – Wurstsalat

Das fränkische Mundartwort meint mit „Gwerch" ein Durcheinander, in diesem Fall die Mischung verschiedener Wurstspezialitäten, von denen es in Franken zahlreiche gibt. Es sind auch Rezepte mit anderen Wurstsorten zu finden, wichtig ist jedoch, dass immer Ochsenmaulsalat dabei ist.
Stadtwurst ist eine der beliebtesten Brühwurstsorten in Franken, es gibt sie in drei Sorten: weiß, rot (meist geräuchert) und schwarz.

1 weiße Zwiebel
1 rote Zwiebel
200 g weißer Presskopf (heller Schwartenmagen mit Fleisch vom Schweinekopf; alternativ eine ungeräucherte, grobstückige Schweinepresswurst)
200 g roter Presskopf (Presswurst mit Schweineblut; alternativ eine feste, grobstückige Blutwurst)
200 g Stadtwurst (alternativ eine andere grobe Brühwurst oder gerauchte Schinkenwurst)
200 g Ochsenmaulsalat (vom Metzger; alternativ gepökelte Ochsenzunge)
100 g Presssack (geräucherte Blutwurst im Naturdarm bzw. Schweinemagen; alternativ eine andere, feste, geräucherte grobstückige Blutwurst)

Marinade
3 EL Salatöl
4 EL Apfelessig
½ TL Salz
1 Prise Zucker
weißer Pfeffer, frisch gemahlen

4 Radieschen
2 Tomaten
1 großes Bund Schnittlauch (ca. 50 g)
1 kleiner Kopfsalat

Zwiebeln schälen und in feine Ringer schneiden. Würste häuten und in dünne Streifen schneiden. Zusammen mit dem Ochsenmaulsalat und den Zwiebelringen in eine Glasschüssel geben.
Für die Marinade Öl, Essig, Salz, Zucker und etwas weißen Pfeffer mit einem Schneebesen gut vermischen. Zur Wurst und den Zwiebeln geben und vermengen.
Radieschen waschen, trockentupfen und raspeln. Tomaten waschen, in Achtel schneiden und Strunk entfernen. Schnittlauch in feine Röllchen schneiden. Blätter vom Kopfsalat zupfen, waschen und trockenschleudern.
Radieschen und Tomaten zum Wurstsalat geben. Eine Platte mit schönen Kopfsalatblättern auslegen, Gwerch darauf anrichten und mit Schnittlauchröllchen überstreuen.
Dazu schmecken frische Brötchen (in Franken: Weggla) oder Bauernbrot.

Nuremberg Mess – Sausage Salad

In the local Franconian dialect, "Gwerch" means a mess, in this case a mix of different kinds of speciality sausage, of which there is a great variety in Franconia. There are recipes which use different kinds of sausages, but the important thing is to always include ox-cheek salad.
Stadtwurst or "city sausage" is the most popular kind of boiled sausage in Franconia. There are three types: white, red (mostly smoked), and black.

1 white onion
1 red onion
8 oz white "Presskopf" (light pork brawn), alternatively, unsmoked chunks of "Schweinepresswurst" (pressed pork sausage)
8 oz red "Schweinepresswurst" (pressed pork sausage with pig's blood), alternatively, chunks of blood sausage
8 oz "Stadtwurst", alternatively, any coarse boiled sausage or smoked ham sausage
8 oz ox-cheek salad (from the butcher), alternatively, cured ox-tongue
4 oz "Presssack" (smoked blood sausage in either natural casing or pig stomach), alternatively, any other firm, smoked, blood sausage in chunks

Marinade
3 tbsp salad oil
4 tbsp cider vinegar
½ tsp salt
1 pinch sugar
white pepper, freshly milled

4 radishes
2 tomatoes
1 large bunch of chives (approx. 2 oz)
1 small head of lettuce

Peel the onions and slice into thin rings. Skin the sausages and slice thinly.
Place the sausages in a glass bowl together with the ox-cheek salad and the onion rings.
For the marinade: using a whisk, thoroughly mix the oil, vinegar, sugar and some white pepper.
Pour the marinade over the sausage and onions, then mix well.
Wash and dry the radishes, then slice finely using a grater.
Wash the tomatoes, remove the greenish stalk base and cut them into eight pieces. Finely chop the chives.
Separate the lettuce leaves, wash them, then dry well in a salad spinner.
Add the radishes and tomatoes to the sausage salad.
Arrange the lettuce on a serving platter, place the "Gwerch" on the lettuce leaves and decorate with the chives.
Serve with fresh bread rolls (in Franken: Weggla), or farmer's bread.

Coburger Zwiebelfleisch
Coburg Meat and Onion Salad

Coburger Zwiebelfleisch

Diese herzhafte Brotzeit ist eine beliebte, regionale Spezialität. Im Sommer schmeckt sie zu einem kernigen Stück Brot, im Winter zu knusprigen Bratkartoffeln. Statt Schweinebauch lässt sich auch kaltes Bratenfleisch dafür verwenden. Reste sind ohne weiteres einige Tage im Kühlschrank haltbar.

2 weiße Zwiebeln
2 rote Zwiebeln
¼ l Wasser
3 EL milder Weinessig
3 EL Salatöl
500 g Schweinebauch, gekocht und gepökelt, vom Metzger in dünne Scheiben geschnitten
2 Gewürzgurken
5 Radieschen
2 Tomaten
¼ Bund krause Petersilie
Salz und schwarzer Pfeffer, frisch gemahlen

Zwiebeln schälen und in feine Ringe schneiden. Wasser aufkochen und Zwiebelringe damit einige Minuten überbrühen. Weinessig und Öl dazugeben und alles in eine flache Schale gießen, abkühlen lassen.
Schweinebauch schichtartig abwechselnd mit Zwiebelringen und dünnen Gewürzgurkenscheiben in die abgekühlte Marinade einlegen. Abgedeckt in den Kühlschrank stellen und einige Stunden durchziehen lassen.
Radieschen, Tomaten und Petersilie waschen. Radieschen entweder fein hobeln oder in dünne Stifte schneiden. Tomaten in Achtel schneiden und den Strunk entfernen. Petersilie ohne Stiel fein hacken und unter das Zwiebelfleisch mischen. Mit Radieschen und Tomaten garnieren, mit Salz und Pfeffer abschmecken.
Dazu passt ein fein gewürztes fränkisches Steinofenbrot aus Natursauerteig.

Volkacher Weinsuppe

Die Volkacher Mainschleife bietet ein optimales Klima für Wein-, Spargel- und Obstanbau. Jährlich Mitte August findet dort das größte Weinfest Frankens statt. Auch hier wird – wie in vielen anderen Weingegenden – Wein nicht nur zum Trinken, sondern gerne zum Kochen verwendet.

3 Schalotten, 3 EL Butter
½ l Hühnerbrühe
½ l Frankenwein, z.B. Silvaner
1 EL Mehl
¼ l Sahne/Rahm
1 Prise Muskatnuss, frisch gerieben
Salz
1 Prise weißer Pfeffer
2 Eigelbe, verquirlt
2 Toastbrotscheiben
1 Prise Zimtpulver

Schalotten schälen und in kleine Würfel schneiden. 1 EL Butter in einem Topf erhitzen, Schalottenwürfel darin bei mittlerer Temperatur glasig anschwitzen. Mit Brühe ablöschen, Hitze erhöhen und fünf Minuten köcheln lassen. Danach die Bouillon durch ein Sieb in einen Topf abgießen. Wein zugießen und solange ohne Deckel kochen, bis sie um ungefähr ein Drittel reduziert ist.
In einer kleinen Pfanne 1 EL Butter erhitzen, Mehl darüberstäuben und zu einer hellen Mehlschwitze glatt verrühren. Diese mit einem Schneebesen unter die Flüssigkeit schlagen und solange rühren, bis die Suppe eine cremige Konsistenz bekommt. Sahne hineinrühren und mit Muskat, etwas Salz und weißem Pfeffer abschmecken. Topf vom Herd nehmen und Eigelbe unterziehen. Die Suppe darf dabei nicht mehr kochen.
Toastbrot klein würfeln, in einer Pfanne in der restlichen Butter unter ständigem Wenden goldbraun braten.
Suppe anrichten, mit Croûtons und etwas Zimt bestreuen und sogleich servieren.

Coburg Meat and Onion Salad

This hearty snack is a popular regional speciality. In summer, it tastes great served with a chunk of bread; in winter, with crispy roast potatoes. Instead of using pork belly, you can also use cold roast pork, since left-overs keep for days in the fridge.

2 white onions
2 red onions
½ pint water
3 tbsp mild wine vinegar
3 tbsp salad oil
1 lb pork belly, boiled and cured (have it sliced finely at the butcher's)
2 gherkins
5 radishes
2 tomatoes
¼ bunch of curly parsley
salt and black pepper, freshly milled

Peel the onions and cut into thin rings. Boil the water and pour it over the onion rings. Leave to stand for a few minutes. Add the onion vinegar and the oil and pour everything into a shallow bowl. Leave to cool.
When cool, layer the sliced pork belly, onion rings and finely sliced gherkins in the dish with the cooled marinade. Cover and place in the fridge. Leave to marinate for a few hours.
Wash the radishes, tomatoes and parsley. Finely slice the radishes, or cut them into fine strips. Remove the green stalk base from the tomatoes and cut them into eight wedges. Finely chop the parsley, including the stems, and add it to the onions and meat. Garnish with radishes and tomatoes, and season with salt and pepper.
Serve with stone-oven baked sour-dough bread.

Volkach Wine Soup

The Volkacher meander is a bend on the River Main, and offers an ideal climate for growing wine, asparagus and fruit. Every year, in mid-August, they hold Franken's largest wine festival. As in many other wine growing areas, the local wine is not just for drinking, it's used for cooking too.

3 shallots, 3 tbsp butter
1 pint chicken stock
1 pint wine from Franconia, e.g., Silvaner
1 tbsp flour
½ pint cream
1 pinch of freshly ground nutmeg
salt
1 pinch of white pepper
2 lightly beaten egg yolks
2 slices of toast bread
1 pinch of cinnamon

Peel the shallots and dice finely. Heat 1 tbsp of butter in a saucepan, and glaze the diced shallots at medium heat until they are transparent. Deglaze with the chicken stock, then increase the heat and leave to simmer for about 5 minutes. Pour the stock through a sieve into a different saucepan. Pour in the wine and boil without a lid until the liquid has reduced by about one third. Heat 1 tbsp of butter in a small frying pan, sprinkle in the flour and stir to make a smooth roux. Using a whisk, stir this into the liquid and keep stirring until the soup has a creamy consistency. Add the cream, then season with nutmeg, a little salt, and white pepper. Remove the saucepan from the heat and stir in the egg yolk. The soup must be below boiling point when you do this. Cut the toast bread into cubes and place them in a frying pan with the remaining butter. Fry until golden brown.
Serve the soup with the croutons and a sprinkling of cinnamon.

Schnitz mit Baggala
Vegetable Stew with Potato Fritters

Schnitz mit Baggala – Gemüseeintopf mit Kartoffelpuffern

Dies ist das „Nationalgericht" der oberfränkischen Stadt Hof an der Saale, Schnitz und Baggala werden aber auch im Umkreis und im Frankenwald gerne gegessen. Von den Zutaten und der Konsistenz kann die Suppe nach persönlicher Vorliebe variieren. Die Baggala aus rohem Kartoffelteig schmecken nicht nur zu Schnitz, sondern auch zu Räucherlachs, Quark, Apfelmus oder Kompott.

2 Zwiebeln
¼ Knollensellerie
4 große Kartoffeln
1 Kohlrabi
6 Karotten
2 Stangen Lauch
1 kleiner Blumenkohl
300 g Stangenbohnen
1 EL Butter
2 l Fleischbrühe (siehe Tipp), erhitzt; alternativ: Gemüsebrühe
1 TL Majoran, getrocknet oder frisch gehackte Blätter
2 Lorbeerblätter
1 TL Liebstöckel, getrocknet oder frisch gehackte Blättchen
½ Bund Petersilie
Salz und schwarzer Pfeffer, frisch gemahlen

Baggala:

6 große Kartoffeln, vorwiegend festkochend, geschält
½ kleine Zwiebel, geschält
4 EL Quark
1 Ei
1 TL Essig
Salz und weißer Pfeffer, frisch gemahlen
4 EL Öl zum Braten

Gemüse küchenfertig vorbereiten: alles putzen und waschen, nach Bedarf schälen, vom Lauch die äußeren Blätter entfernen, von den Bohnen beide Enden kappen. Zwiebeln und Sellerie in feine Würfel schneiden, Kartoffeln, Kohlrabi und Karotten in mundgerechte Stücke. Lauch in Streifen schneiden. Strunk beim Blumenkohl herausschneiden und anderweitig verwenden. Röschen des Blumenkohls aufteilen. Bohnen je nach Größe halbieren oder dritteln.
Butter in einem großen Topf erhitzen, Zwiebeln darin anschwitzen. Restliches Gemüse dazugeben und mit der heißen Fleischbrühe auffüllen. Eintopf zum Kochen bringen, mit Majoran, Lorbeerblättern und Liebstöckel würzen. So lange bei mittlerer Temperatur garen, bis das Gemüse noch einen leichten Biss hat.
In der Zwischenzeit für die Baggala Kartoffeln und Zwiebel auf einer feinen Raffel in eine Schüssel reiben. Masse mit Quark, Ei und Essig vermengen, nach Geschmack salzen und pfeffern.
In einer großen antihaft-beschichteten Bratpfanne Öl erhitzen. Pro Baggala einen Schöpflöffel der Kartoffelmasse hineingeben und kross ausbacken. Petersilie waschen, trockentupfen und ohne Stiele fein hacken. Suppe mit Salz und Pfeffer abschmecken. In Suppenteller füllen und mit etwas Petersilie bestreuen.
Die Kartoffelpuffer separat zur Suppe servieren.

Tipp:

Einfache Fleischbrühe selber herstellen aus ca. 1 kg Suppenfleisch (z.B. Ochsenbrust), einigen Suppenknochen und 2 l leicht gesalzenem Wasser. In einem großen Topf aufsetzen und weich kochen, dabei immer wieder den Schaum abschöpfen. Fleisch dann in Scheiben oder Würfel geschnitten zur Suppe geben für eine sättigende Mahlzeit.

Vegetable Stew with Potato Fritters

"Schnitz and Baggala" is considered the "national dish" in the city of Hof an der Saale, which is situated in Upper Franken, although it's also popular throughout the region and in Frankenwald. Depending on the ingredients you use, and your personal taste, the consistency of the soup can vary. The "Baggala", which are a kind of potato fritter made with raw potato dough, don't just taste good with "Schnitz" (which is: the stew), but are also good with smoked salmon, quark, apple sauce or compote.

2 onions
¼ celeriac
4 large potatoes
1 kohlrabi
6 carrots
2 leeks
1 small cauliflower
11 oz runner beans
1 tbsp butter
4 pints meat stock (see tip), heated; alternatively vegetable stock
1 tsp marjoram, dried or freshly chopped leaves
2 bay leaves
1 tsp lovage, dried or freshly chopped leaves
½ bunch of parsley
salt and black pepper, freshly milled

Baggala (potato fritters):
6 large potatoes, peeled
½ small onion, peeled
4 tbsp quark
1 egg
1 tsp vinegar
salt and white pepper, freshly milled
4 tbsp oil for frying

Prepare the vegetables: wash and dry everything, and peel if necessary. Remove the outer layers from the leeks, and top and tail the runner beans. Dice the onions and the celeriac, then cut the potatoes, kohlrabi and carrots into bite sized chunks. Cut the leeks into strips. Remove the stalk from the cauliflower (you can use it for cooking something else later).
Separate the cauliflower into small florets and, depending on how big they are, cut the beans into two or three pieces.
Heat the butter in a large saucepan, and sweat the onions. Add the remaining vegetables along with the hot meat stock. Bring the stew to the boil, and season with the marjoram, bay leaves and lovage. Boil until the vegetables are firm to the bite.
Wash the parsley, then dry and remove the stalks and finely chop the rest.
Season the soup with salt and pepper.
In the meantime, prepare the "Baggala": Grate the potatoes and onions finely into a bowl. Mix with the quark, egg and vinegar and season with salt and pepper.
Heat the oil in a large frying pan. Use a ladle of the mixture for each "Baggala" and fry until crispy. Serve separately to the soup.
Fill the soup into bowls and sprinkle with parsley with a side serving of Baggala.

Tip:
Make your own stock easily using 2 lb of soup meat (e.g. brisket of beef), a few soup bones and 4 pints of lightly salted water. Place everything in a large pan and cook until soft, removing the foam that comes to the surface from time to time with a ladle.
For a filling and satisfying meal, cut the meat into slices or cubes and add to the soup.

Gebackener Karpfen mit lauwarmem Kartoffelsalat
Baked Carp in Batter with Lukewarm Potato Salad

Gebackener Karpfen im Bierteig

Gebackener Karpfen ist sowohl im Fränkischen als auch in der angrenzenden Oberpfalz eine begehrte Spezialität. Man bekommt ihn ab Oktober frisch, wenn die Teiche abgefischt werden. In Franken ragt besonders die Teichwirtschaft des berühmten Aischgrunds heraus. Die Karpfenzucht geht auf die Klöster des frühen Mittelalters zurück. Bekanntlich verzehrten die Mönche den fleischigen Fisch gerne als Fastenspeise und legten deshalb dafür Teiche an, von denen viele heute noch genutzt werden.
Der gebackene Karpfen ist in Franken oft kulinarischer Bestandteil einer Kirchweih, während er an Weihnachten und Silvester auch häufig „blau", also in einem Weinsud (siehe auch Seite 50 „Blausud") gegart, auf den Tisch kommt.

1 Karpfen, ca. 1 ½ kg, küchenfertig und längs halbiert
1 Zitrone, Saft
Salz und Pfeffer, frisch gemahlen

Bierteig:
150 g Mehl
100 ml helles Bier
1 EL Butter, zerlassen
2 große Eier, getrennt
Butterschmalz zum Ausbacken
etwas Mehl zum Wenden
1 Zitrone, geachtelt
1 Bund Petersilie

Karpfenhälften unter fließendem kalten Wasser waschen und mit Küchenkrepp gründlich trockentupfen. Zitronensaft darüberträufeln, danach salzen und pfeffern. Etwa zehn Minuten ziehen lassen.
Währenddessen den Bierteig zubereiten: Mehl mit Bier, flüssiger Butter und Eigelben verquirlen, leicht salzen und den Teig 15 Minuten quellen lassen. Dann das Eiweiß sehr steif schlagen und unter den Teig ziehen.
So viel Butterschmalz in einer tiefen, großen Bratpfanne erhitzen, dass es etwa fingerbreit darin steht.
Karpfenhälften von beiden Seiten im Mehl wenden, abklopfen, durch den Bierteig ziehen und im heißen Fett von beiden Seiten goldbraun ausbacken. Herausnehmen und auf Küchenkrepp abtropfen lassen.
Karpfen mit Zitronenachteln und Petersilie garnieren. Besonders gut schmeckt dazu ein lauwarmer Kartoffelsalat (Rezept, siehe Seite 56).

Baked Carp in Batter

Baked carp is a sought after delicacy both in Franconia and the Upper Palatinate. You can get it fresh from October onwards, when the fish ponds are emptied. In Franconia, the fish farms around Aischgrund are legendary. Carp farming dates back to the monasteries of the Middle Ages. It's a well-known fact that the monks liked to eat this meat-like fish during Lent, and so they created fish ponds especially for breeding carp. Many of them are still in use to this day.
Baked carp is often served at religious festivals in Franconia, whereas at Christmas and New Year it's usually prepared in wine broth (see page 31 and 51*).*

1 carp, approx. 3 lb, cleaned and halved lengthwise
1 lemon (juice only)
salt and pepper, freshly milled

Batter:

5 oz flour
6 tbsp light beer
1 tbsp melted butter
2 large eggs, separated
clarified butter for frying
a little flour for covering the fish
1 lemon, cut into 8 wedges
1 bunch of parsley

Wash the carp under running water and dry well with paper towels. Squeeze the lemon juice over the fish and season with salt and pepper. Leave to marinate for about ten minutes.
In the meantime, prepare the batter: Mix the flour with beer, melted butter and egg yolks. Add a little salt, and leave the batter to rest for 15 minutes. Beat the egg-white until they are stiff and fold them into the batter.
Heat enough clarified butter in the frying pan that the liquid butter is about as deep as the width of your finger.
Roll the carp fillets in flour, shaking off any loose flour, then dip them in the batter and fry on both sides until they are golden brown.
Remove from the pan and drain them on paper towels. Decorate with the lemon wedges and parsley.
This tastes particularly good when served with lukewarm potato salad (recipe on page 57).

Wallerfilet mit Meerrettichhaube
Catfish in Horseradish Crust

Wallerfilet mit Meerrettichhaube

Der Waller oder Wels, wie er eigentlich heißt, ist der größte Süßwasserfisch Europas. Er wird mittlerweile auch im Frankenland in Teichen gezüchtet. Wallerfilet mit Meerrettichhaube ist ein Rezept der neueren Generation. Im Frankenwald wird der Waller oft noch traditionell blau aus dem Sud (siehe auch Seite 50 „Blausud") serviert. Dazu gehören dann Salzkartoffeln und eine deftige Sauce mit Speck, Zwiebeln, Wein und Kräutern.

2 rote Zwiebeln
1 kleine rote Gemüsepaprika
4 EL Butter, zimmerwarm
4 Scheiben Weißbrot ohne Rinde
½ Bund Dill
¼ Bund Petersilie
3 EL Meerrettich, frisch gerieben oder aus dem Glas
Salz und schwarzer Pfeffer, frisch gemahlen
4 Wallerfilets à 200 g
3 EL Butterschmalz
1 Zitrone, Saft

Backofen auf 180 °C vorheizen.
Zwiebeln schälen, in sehr kleine Würfel schneiden. Paprika kurz in kochendes Wasser legen, dann herausnehmen und die Haut abziehen. Stiel und Kerne entfernen, Paprika klein würfeln.
1 EL Butter in einer Pfanne erhitzen, Zwiebel- und Paprikawürfel hineingeben. Etwa fünf Minuten darin anschwitzen, dann abkühlen lassen. Weißbrot in Würfel schneiden. Dill und Petersilie unter fließendem Wasser waschen, trockenschütteln und Stiele entfernen. Blätter fein hacken. Restliche Butter mit der Zwiebel-Paprika-Masse, Kräutern, Weißbrot und Meerrettich verkneten und mit Salz und Pfeffer abschmecken.
Wallerfilets unter kaltem Wasser waschen, mit Küchenkrepp abtupfen. Filets mit Zitronensaft beträufeln und wenige Minuten einziehen lassen. Butterschmalz in einer Pfanne erhitzen, Fischstücke darin von beiden Seiten kurz anbraten. Waller herausnehmen und mit der Hautseite nach oben in eine ofenfeste Form legen. Filets dick mit der Meerrettichmasse bestreichen und im vorgeheizten Backofen auf der mittleren Schiene goldbraun fertiggaren.
Mit Kartoffelpüree servieren oder Scheiben von frischem, knusprigem Weißbrot dazu reichen.

Catfish in Horseradish Crust

The catfish is the largest freshwater fish in Europe, and these days they are also bred in ponds throughout Franken.
Fillet of catfish filet in horseradish crust is one of the newer recipes from the region. In Frankenwald, catfish are still often prepared the traditional way in a wine broth called "Blausud", or "blue broth". The name comes from the fact that when the fish is cooked in this broth, the skin of the fish turns blue. The fish is then served with boiled potatoes, and a hearty sauce made of bacon, onions, wine and herbs.

2 red onions
1 small red bell pepper
4 tbsp butter, at room temperature
4 slices of white bread, without the crusts
½ bunch of dill
¼ bunch of parsley
3 tbsp horseradish, freshly grated or from the jar
salt and black pepper, freshly milled
4 catfish fillets, approx. 8 oz each
3 tbsp clarified butter
1 lemon (juice only)

Preheat the oven to 350°F.
Peel the onions and dice them very finely. Place the bell pepper in boiling water for a moment, then take it out and remove the skin. Remove the stem and the seeds, then dice the flesh too.
Put a tablespoon of butter in a pan together with the onions and bell peppers. Sweat them for about five minutes and leave to cool.
Cut the bread into cubes.
Wash the dill and parsley under running water, shake dry and remove the stalks. Chop finely.
Mix the remaining butter with the onion and bell pepper mixture, herbs, white bread and horseradish, then season with salt and pepper.
Wash the catfish fillets under running water and dry them with paper towels. Pour the lemon juice over the fillets and leave them to marinate for a few minutes.
Heat the clarified butter in a pan and fry the fish briefly on both sides. Remove the catfish fillets and place them in an ovenproof dish with the skin facing up. Spread thickly with the horseradish mixture and bake until golden brown on the middle shelf of the preheated oven.
Serve with mashed potatoes or simply with slices of fresh, crunchy white bread.

Mostgockel mit Serviettkloß
Franconian "Coq au Vin" with Napkin Dumpling

Mostgockel

Mainfranken ist Weinfranken! Mit Most ist hier die Vorstufe zum Wein gemeint, der auch als Federweißer oder Bremser bezeichnet wird. Man bekommt ihn nur wenige Wochen im Frühherbst. Weil der Mostgockel aber auch zu jeder anderen Jahreszeit schmeckt, kann er alternativ mit einem jungen Weißwein zubereitet werden.

1 großes Hähnchen oder 1 Poularde, ausgenommen und küchenfertig
1 l gegorener Traubenmost (Federweißer oder Federroter) oder junger Frankenwein
6 Schalotten
2 Knoblauchzehen
150 g durchwachsener Speck
Salz und Pfeffer, frisch gemahlen
70 g Butter
2 Lorbeerblätter
2 TL Estragon, getrocknet
1 EL Paprikapulver
1 TL Thymian, getrocknet
1 EL Weinbrand
2 EL Mehl

Geflügel waschen, in portionsgerechte Stücke zerteilen und in eine Schüssel legen. Most darübergießen und für einige Stunden abgedeckt in den Kühlschrank stellen.
Schalotten und Knoblauch schälen und sehr fein hacken. Speck in kleine Würfel schneiden und in einer Pfanne goldbraun anbraten. Knoblauch und Schalotten hinzufügen und ca. fünf Minuten darin anschwitzen.
Hähnchenteile aus der Marinade nehmen, trockentupfen, leicht salzen und pfeffern. In einem großen Bräter die Hälfte der Butter erhitzen und die Geflügelstücke darin von allen Seiten braun anbraten. Fleisch herausheben und Bratensatz mit der durchgeseihten Marinade ablöschen. Speck, Schalotten, Knoblauch sowie Lorbeerblätter, Estragon, Paprikapulver und Thymian dazugeben. Aufkochen lassen und die Hähnchenteile wieder einlegen. Etwa 50 Minuten schmoren lassen, dann das Fleisch wieder herausnehmen.
Garflüssigkeit aufkochen lassen. Mehl mit etwas kaltem Wasser verrühren und die Sauce damit binden. Mit Weinbrand abschmecken, nach Geschmack salzen und pfeffern. Geflügel im Bräter weitere zehn Minuten ziehen lassen.
Zu diesem mainfränkischen Gericht passt der Serviettkloß (Seite 60) oder Salzkartoffeln und frische Salate als Beilage.

Franconian "Coq au Vin"

Mainfranken is "Wine Franken"! "Most", or "must" as we call it in English, is the name given to wine in the early stages of the wine making process. In Franconia, it's also known as "Federweißer" or "Bremser". It's only available for a few weeks in early Fall, but since "Mostgockel" tastes good all year round, it can be prepared using a young white wine instead.

1 large chicken or poularde (oven-ready)
2 pints of fermented red or white grape must (Federweißer or Federroter), or a young Franconian wine
6 shallots
2 cloves of garlic
5 oz streaky bacon
salt and pepper, freshly milled
2½ oz butter
2 bay leaves
2 tsp tarragon, dried
1 tbsp paprika powder
1 tbsp thyme dried
1 tbsp brandy
2 tbsp flour

Wash the chicken, then cut it into serving sized portions and place them in a bowl. Pour in the must so that it covers the chicken, cover the dish with a lid, and cool in the fridge for a few hours. Peel the shallots and garlic, then chop them very finely. Dice the bacon into small cubes. Brown the bacon in a frying pan until the fat has melted, then add the onions and garlic, and sweat for about five minutes.
Remove the chicken pieces from the marinade and dry with paper towels.
Season them with a little salt and some pepper.
Pour the marinade through a sieve. Heat half of the butter in a large casserole dish, then fry the chicken pieces until golden brown all over.
Remove the meat from the frying pan.
Deglaze the pan with the marinade, then add the bacon, shallots, garlic, bay leaves, tarragon, paprika powder and thyme.
Bring everything to the boil, then add the chicken pieces again. Simmer for about 50 minutes, then remove the meat once again.
Bring the liquid in the casserole dish to the boil.
Mix the flour with cold water and bind the sauce.
Add brandy to taste, and season with salt and pepper.
Put the chicken back in the casserole dish and leave to simmer for a further ten minutes.
This Main Franconian speciality goes with napkin dumplings (page 61) or with boiled potatoes and fresh salad.

Spargel mit fränkischen Bratwürsten
Asparagus with Franconian Grilling Sausages

Spargel mit fränkischen Bratwürsten

Fränkischer Spargel hat eine lange Tradition und einen guten Ruf. In den drei fränkischen Regierungsbezirken liegen über 40 % der gesamten bayerischen Spargelanbauflächen.
Bratwürste sind das Aushängeschild fränkischer Metzgereien und regional höchst unterschiedlich in Größe und Konsistenz.

2 kg weißer Stangenspargel
3 l Wasser
1 unbehandelte Bio-Zitrone, geviertelt
250 g Butter, 2 TL Salz
1 TL Zucker, 1 Lorbeerblatt
2 kg kleine fest kochende Kartoffeln
1 TL Öl zum Braten
4 Paar frische, fränkische Bratwürste
¼ l Milch, erhitzt
1 EL Schnittlauchröllchen

Spargel gründlich schälen, die holzigen Enden entfernen. Wasser in einem hohen weiten Topf auf den Herd setzen. Ein Zitronenviertel mit 50 g Butter, Salz, Zucker und Lorbeerblatt dazugeben. Aufkochen, Spargel einlegen, ca. 20 Minuten köcheln lassen. Zitrone nach zehn Minuten entfernen. Der Spargel ist fertig, wenn er noch einen leichten Biss hat.
In der Zwischenzeit Kartoffeln schälen und in einem Topf mit ungefähr 2 l Wasser weichkochen. Je nach Größe dauert das ca. 15 Minuten.
Restliche Butter in einer kleinen Pfanne erhitzen und leicht bräunen.
Bratwürste kurz in heißer Milch schwenken und mit Küchenkrepp abtupfen. Dann spritzen und platzen sie nicht so schnell, wenn sie im erhitzten Öl in einer Eisenpfanne bei mittlerer Temperatur gebraten werden.
Kartoffeln abseihen und je drei mit einem Paar Bratwürsten sowie fünf bis sechs Stangen Spargel auf einem vorgewärmten Teller anrichten. Spargel mit der gebräunten Butter übergießen und mit Schnittlauch bestreuen.

Schäufele aus dem Rohr

Schäufele gehören auch in Franken zu den Traditionsgerichten. Meist werden sie mit Kartoffelklößen (Halbseidene Klöße, siehe Seite 56) und Sauerkraut serviert.

4 Schäufele (Schweineschulter mit Knochen und Schwarte)
Salz
schwarzer Pfeffer, frisch gemahlen
ca. 200 ml Wasser
2 Zwiebeln
3 Knoblauchzehen
2 Karotten
1 große Stange Lauch
1 l Gemüsebrühe, heiß
1 EL Kümmelsamen

Backofen auf 220 °C vorheizen.
Fleischstücke waschen und abtrocknen. Von allen Seiten kräftig mit Salz und Pfeffer einreiben, bis auf die Schwarte, die nur gesalzen wird.
Schäufele mit der Schwarte nach oben in einen Bräter stellen und Wasser zugießen. In den vorgeheizten Backofen schieben und 30 Minuten braten.
In der Zwischenzeit das Gemüse vorbereiten: Zwiebeln, Knoblauch und Karotten schälen und grob hacken. Lauch waschen und in große Stücke schneiden.
Bräter aus dem Ofen nehmen, Gemüse um die Schäufele garnieren, heiße Gemüsebrühe zugießen und den Kümmel darauf verteilen. Zurück in den Ofen stellen und dort ca. zwei Stunden braten. Dabei die Schäufele immer im Auge behalten und alle halbe Stunde mit Bratflüssigkeit begießen. Sobald das Fleisch beginnt, sich vom Knochen zu lösen und die Schwarte kross und knusprig braun geworden ist, sind die Schäufele fertig. Sauce durch ein Sieb abseihen, abschmecken und dazu servieren.

Asparagus with Franconian Grilling Sausages

Asparagus has a long tradition in Franconia, and a good reputation too. Over 40 % of Bavaria's asparagus farming land lies within the three Franconian administrative districts. Grilling sausages are the leading product of Franconia's butchers and can vary greatly in size and consistency.

4 lb white asparagus spears
6 pints water
1 unwaxed lemon, quartered
9 oz butter, 1 tsp salt, 1 tsp sugar
1 bay leaf
4 lb waxy potatoes
1 tsp oil for frying
4 pairs fresh, Franconian grilling sausages
½ pint milk, heated
1 tbsp chopped chives

Peel the asparagus well and remove the woody ends. Put the water in a tall, wide saucepan, and place on the heat. Add ¼ lemon, 2 oz butter, salt, sugar and the bay leaf, then bring to the boil. Add the asparagus and leave to simmer for about 20 minutes.
Remove the lemon after ten minutes. The asparagus is ready when it's still firm to the bite.
In the meantime, peel the potatoes. Cook until soft in a saucepan with about four pints of water. Depending on how big the potatoes are, this will take about 15 minutes.
Heat the rest of the butter in a small frying pan until slightly browned.
Dip the grilling sausages in the milk and dry them with kitchen paper. This helps prevent the fat from spitting when you place them in the pan. They don't burst as easily when they are fried in an iron griddle pan at medium heat.
Drain the potatoes. Serve three potatoes with a pair of sausages, and five or six spears of asparagus on a preheated plate. Pour the browned butter over the asparagus and garnish with chives.

Oven Roast Pork Shoulder

Oven roast pork shoulder is a traditional dish, which you can find in several regions troughout Germany. In Franconia, it is mostly served with potato dumplings (Silky Dumplings, see page 57) and sauerkraut.

4 pork shoulders (with bones and rind)
salt
black pepper, freshly milled
approx. ½ pint water
2 onions
3 cloves of garlic
2 carrots
1 long leek
2 pints vegetable stock, hot
1 tbsp caraway seeds

Preheat the oven to 430°F.
Wash and dry the meat. Rub all over with plenty of salt and pepper, apart from the rinds, where you should only use salt. Place the pork shoulders, with the rinds facing upward in a roasting pan and add the water. Place in the preheated oven and roast for 30 minutes.
In the meantime, prepare the vegetables. Peel the onions, garlic and carrots, then chop roughly. Wash the leek and cut it into large chunks.
Remove the roasting pan from the oven, garnish the meat with the vegetables, and pour in the vegetable stock. Sprinkle with the caraway seeds. Put back in the oven and roast for two hours. Keep an eye on the shoulders and baste with the juice every 30 minutes. The meat is done as soon as the meat begins to come off the bone and the rinds have turned crispy and brown.
Pour the sauce through a sieve, season to taste and serve with the meat.

Schäufele aus dem Rohr
Oven Roast Pork Shoulder

Sauerbraten mit dunkler Sauce

Saucenlebkuchen ist ein einfacher, nur schwach gesüßter Lebkuchen, der speziell zum Kochen produziert wird und überwiegend regional zu bekommen ist. Als Ersatz können auch einfache Printen oder Lebkuchen ohne Glasur oder Schokolade verwendet werden.

Marinade:

$^1/_8$ l Weinessig
1 Lorbeerblatt
6 Pfefferkörner
4 Pimentkörner
4 Wacholderbeeren
1 l Wasser

2 kg Rindfleisch zum Braten, am besten aus Keule oder Schulter
1 Karotte
¼ Knollensellerie
2 Zwiebeln
3 EL Öl zum Braten
1 l klare Gemüsebrühe
1–2 Saucenlebkuchen
ca. $^1/_8$ l Wasser
1 EL Kirschgelee
1 EL Butter
2 EL Rotwein
Salz und schwarzer Pfeffer, frisch gemahlen

Alle Zutaten für die Marinade in einem Topf aufkochen und wieder abkühlen lassen. Flüssigkeit in eine Porzellanschüssel gießen.
Fleisch unter kaltem Wasser waschen und mit Küchenkrepp trockentupfen. In die Flüssigkeit einlegen und abgedeckt über Nacht im Kühlschrank darin marinieren. Am nächsten Tag das Rindfleisch herausnehmen und gründlich trockentupfen.
Von allen Seiten mit Salz und Pfeffer einreiben.
Gemüse und Zwiebeln schälen und in grobe Stücke hacken.
Öl in einem Bräter erhitzen und das Fleisch darin kräftig anbraten. Zwiebeln und Gemüse dazugeben, mit der Hälfte der abgeseihten Marinade und der Gemüsebrühe ablöschen. Deckel auf den Bräter legen und das Fleisch darin ca. zwei Stunden schmoren lassen.
Sobald das Fleisch gar ist, aus dem Bräter heben. Schmorgemüse mit Flüssigkeit durch ein Spitzsieb passieren. Lebkuchen in kaltem Wasser einweichen, verquirlen und zur Sauce geben. Diese zurück in den Bräter geben und aufkochen lassen, bis sie sämig wird. Jetzt Kirschgelee, Butter und Rotwein unterrühren, mit Salz und Pfeffer abschmecken.
Fleisch zurück in die Sauce legen und bei geringer Hitze darin noch 20 Minuten ziehen lassen.
Klassische Beilagen sind Blaukraut und hausgemachte Klöße. Besonders fein schmeckt ein Serviettkloß (Rezept, siehe Seite 60) dazu, der in Scheiben geschnitten auf dem Teller angerichtet wird.

Marinated Pot Roast in Dark Sauce

Cooking gingerbread is a simple, slightly less sweet version of the original, which is produced in the region especially for cooking. Since it is hard to come by elsewhere, standard gingerbread cookies (without chocolate or sugar coating!) can be used instead.

Marinade:

¼ pint wine vinegar
1 bay leaf
6 peppercorns
4 allspice berries
4 juniper berries
2 pints water

4 lbs beef for roasting, haunch or shoulder
1 carrot
¼ celeriac
2 onions
3 tbsp oil for frying
2 pints clear vegetable stock
1–2 gingerbread cookies for cooking
approx. ¼ pint water
1 tbsp cherry jam
1 tbsp butter
2 tbsp red wine
salt and black pepper, freshly milled

Bring all the ingredients for the marinade to the boil in a saucepan and leave to cool. Pour into a porcelain dish.

Wash the meat under running water and dry with paper towels. Place the meat in the marinade, cover and leave to marinate in the refrigerator overnight. The next day, remove the beef and dry it thoroughly. Rub the meat all over with salt and pepper.

Peel the onions and the vegetables, then cut them into chunks.

Heat the oil in a roasting pan and sear the beef all over. Add the onions and the vegetables to the pan and deglaze using half of the strained marinade, together with the vegetable stock. Place a lid on the roasting pan, and braise the meat for about two hours. As soon as the meat is cooked, remove it from the roasting pan.

Pass the braised vegetables and the juice through a strainer. Soften the gingerbread in cold water, mix to a paste and add to the sauce. Pour this all back into the roasting pan and boil until the mixture has a creamy consistency. Now stir in the cherry jam, butter and red wine. Season with salt and pepper.

Place the meat back in the sauce and simmer over a low heat for another 20 minutes.

Traditional side dishes are red cabbage and homemade dumplings called "Serviettkloß" (napkin dumpling, recipe on page 61).They are particularly good when sliced and served on a plate with the meat.

Kärrnerbraten Würzburger Art
Würzburg Cartman's Roast

Kärrnerbraten Würzburger Art

Als Kärrner bezeichnete man früher die einfachen Fuhrleute, die Waren mit einer „Karre" transportierten. Sie hatten stets großen Appetit und schätzten einen deftigen und satt machenden Braten. Der Kärrnerbraten ist eine regionale Spezialität aus der Würzburger Gegend.

2½ kg Rinderbrust, vom Metzger vorbereitet mit einem Taschenschnitt

Füllung:

4 altbackene Brötchen
6 Schalotten, geschält
2 EL Butter
2 Bund Petersilie
250 g Bratwurstbrät
3 Eier

2 Karotten
100 g Knollensellerie
2 kleine Stangen Lauch
2½ l Wasser, leicht gesalzen
2 Lorbeerblätter
4 Wacholderbeeren
6 Pfefferkörner

2 EL Butter
300 ml Sahne/Rahm
200 ml fränkischer Silvaner
3 EL Mehl
2 EL Tomatenmark
Salz und schwarzer Pfeffer, frisch gemahlen

Fleisch unter kaltem Wasser abspülen und gründlich trocken tupfen. Innen salzen und pfeffern, außen nur leicht salzen.
Für die Füllung Brötchen in etwas kaltem Wasser einweichen. Schalotten schälen, vier Stück davon würfeln und in einer Pfanne ca. fünf Minuten in heißer Butter anschwitzen. Petersilie waschen, trockenschütteln und die Hälfte davon ohne Stiele fein hacken. Zwei bis drei Stängel für die Garnitur beiseite legen.
Brötchen ausdrücken, auseinander zupfen und in eine Schüssel geben. Gehackte Petersilie, Schalottenwürfel, Bratwurstbrät und Eier zu den Brötchen geben und gründlich vermengen. Die Fleischtasche damit füllen und mit Küchengarn zunähen.
Karotten und Sellerie schälen, Lauch waschen. Gemüse grob zerkleinern.
Salzwasser in einem großen Topf aufkochen. Übrige Petersilie und Schalotten, Lorbeerblätter, Wacholderbeeren und Pfefferkörner mit dem Gemüse hinzufügen. Nach fünf Minuten das Fleisch einlegen. Einmal aufkochen lassen, dann die Hitze reduzieren und eine Stunde auf kleinster Stufe garen.
Backofen auf 220°C vorheizen.
Fleisch aus dem Topf heben und abtupfen. Brühe durch ein feines Sieb abgießen und beiseite stellen. Butter in einem Bräter erhitzen und die Rinderbrust darin von allen Seiten kräftig anbraten. Von der Brühe ca. 1 l abschöpfen, mit Sahne vermischen und über das Fleisch gießen. Bräter für 45 Minuten auf der untersten Schiene in den vorgeheizten Backofen stellen.
Fleisch aus dem Bräter heben und auf ein Brett legen. Bratfond durch ein feines Sieb gießen und in einem Topf aufkochen lassen. Wein und Mehl glattrühren, mit dem Tomatenmark vermengen und zum Bratfond geben. Solange erhitzen, bis die Sauce sämig ist. Blättchen der beiseite gelegten Petersilie fein hacken und zur Sauce geben. Mit Salz und Pfeffer abschmecken.
Braten vorsichtig in nicht zu dünne Scheiben aufschneiden, auf Tellern platzieren und großzügig mit Sauce übergießen. Dazu passen Salzkartoffeln und ein frischer Salat.

Würzburg Cartman's Roast – Kärrner Style

"Kärrner" was the name given to simple cartmen who used to transport goods with a cart or barrow. These men always had a good appetite and appreciated a hearty and filling roast. The cartman's roast is a regional speciality from the area around Würzburg.

5 lb beef brisket with a pouch for the stuffing (prepared by the butcher)

Filling:

4 old bread rolls
6 shallots, peeled
2 tbsp butter
2 bunches parsley
9 oz sausage meat
3 eggs

2 carrots
4 oz celeriac
2 small leeks
5 pints of water, slightly salted
2 bay leaves
4 juniper berries
6 peppercorns

2 tbsp butter
⅔ pint cream
approx. ½ pint Franconian Silvaner
3 tbsp flour
2 tbsp tomato puree
salt and black pepper, freshly milled

Rinse the meat under cold running water and dry it thoroughly. Season from the inside with salt and pepper – only use a little salt on the outside of the meat.
For the filling, soak the bread rolls in a little cold water. Peel the shallots. Dice four of them, place in a pan and sweat in hot butter for five minutes.
Wash the parsley, shake it dry and finely chop half of it (without the stalks). Set two or three stalks aside for the garnish.
Squeeze out the bread rolls, tear them into small pieces and place them in a bowl. Add the chopped parsley, diced shallots, sausage meat, and eggs and mix thoroughly. Stuff the beef pouch with the filling, and sew closed using kitchen twine.
Peel the carrots and the celeriac, and wash the leeks. Chop the vegetables into chunks.
Boil the salt water in a saucepan. Add the rest of the parsley, shallots, bay leaves, juniper berries, peppercorns and the vegetables. After five minutes, add the meat. Bring to the boil again, then reduce the heat and simmer at the lowest possible temperature for an hour.
Preheat the oven to 430°F.
Remove the meat from the saucepan and dry with paper towels. Pass the stock through a strainer and put to one side.
Heat the butter in a roasting pan and sear the meat hard on all sides. Take approximately two pints of the stock, mix with the cream and pour over the meat. Place the roasting pan in the preheated oven, on the lowest shelf, for 45 minutes.
Remove the meat from the roasting pan and place it on a chopping board. Pour the roasting juices through a fine strainer and bring to the boil. Mix the wine and the flour to form a smooth paste. Add the tomato puree and stir into the stock. Heat until the sauce has a creamy consistency. Chop the remaining parsley leaves and add to the sauce. Season with salt and pepper.
Carefully, cut the roast into slices that are not too thin. Put them on plates and pour a generous amount of sauce over them.
Serve with boiled potatoes and fresh salad.

Blaue Zibfl
Boiled Sausages in Wine Broth

Blaue Zibfl – Frische Bratwürste im Blausud

Blaue Zibfl werden in der warmen Jahreszeit gerne als Zwischenmahlzeit oder zur Brotzeit gereicht. Die Zubereitung mit Essig und Wein, dem so genannten Blausud, bewirkt eine leichte Art der Konservierung. Meist werden sie mit kräftigem Landbrot, z. B. vom Frankenlaib, serviert. Dieses Rezept stammt von Christine Jaeger, der Wirtin vom „Gasthof zum Falken" in Mainbernheim.

Sud:

6 Wacholderbeeren
2 Lorbeerblätter
6 Pfefferkörner
¼ l weißer Weinessig
¼ l fränkischer Silvaner
¼ l Wasser
½ TL Zucker
¼ TL Salz
2 Zwiebeln
150 g Sellerie
3 Karotten
200 g Lauch

4–6 Paar grobe, fränkische Bratwürste

Wacholderbeeren, Lorbeer und Pfeffer in ein Gewürzsäckchen packen und zum Sud geben, der aus Essig, Wein, Wasser, Zucker und Salz erstellt wird.
Zwiebeln häuten und in Ringe schneiden. Sellerie und Karotten schälen, Lauch waschen. Gemüse in sehr feine Streifen schneiden (eine Julienne bereiten).
Julienne-Gemüse in der Brühe kurz aufkochen, dann den Topf vom Herd ziehen. Würste einlegen und das Ganze bei geringer Hitzezufuhr ca. 20 Minuten simmern lassen.
Mit Salz und Pfeffer abschmecken. Jeweils ein Paar Würste zusammen mit dem Gemüse und seiner Garflüssigkeit in tiefen Tellern anrichten oder alles in einer Suppenterrine servieren.

Kulmbacher Bier-Haxn

Die Dichte an Brauereien ist in Oberfranken besonders hoch. Die Kulmbacher Bierwoche Ende Juli ist eines der größten Bierfeste Deutschlands.

4 Vorderhaxen vom Schwein
Salz und Pfeffer, frisch gemahlen
6 Wacholderbeeren
2 Zwiebeln, 1 Knoblauchzehe
100 g Butterschmalz

1 l Fleischbrühe
½ l dunkles Bier
1 TL Kümmelpulver
1 TL Majoran, gerebelt
¼ TL Thymian, getrocknet

Kartoffelmehl, nach Geschmack

Backofen auf 200°C vorheizen.
Schweinshaxen unter kaltem Wasser waschen und trockentupfen. Mit Salz, Pfeffer und zerdrücktem Wacholder einreiben und 30 Minuten einziehen lassen.
Zwiebeln und Knoblauch schälen, beides fein hacken. Fett in einem Bräter erhitzen, Fleisch darin mit Zwiebeln und Knoblauch rundherum anbraten. Mit Fleischbrühe und etwas Bier ablöschen, Bratensatz mit einem Schaber lösen und die restlichen Gewürze dazugeben.
Offenen Bräter etwa zwei Stunden im Backofen belassen. Das Fleisch zwischendurch mehrmals mit Bier begießen. Falls die Kruste zu dunkel wird, rechtzeitig mit Alufolie abdecken.
Gegarte Haxen aus dem Bräter heben und auf vorgewärmte Teller geben. Sauce durch ein Sieb abseihen, eventuell noch etwas Brühe zugießen. Nach Geschmack die Sauce klar oder leicht abgebunden servieren. Sämiger wird sie durch etwas in kaltem Wasser glattgerührtes Kartoffelmehl. Die Sauce dann nochmals aufkochen.
Sauerkraut und Kartoffelklöße (Halbseidene, siehe Seite 56) passen hervorragend dazu.

Blue Zibfl – Boiled Sausages in Wine Broth

During the warmer months of the year, "Blue Zibfl" are popular between meals or as a snack. Because they are prepared with vinegar and wine broth (the so called "Blausud", means blue broth, see page 31), which acts as a light preservative, they keep well. They are mostly served with a fresh slice of Frankenlaib.
This recipe is from Christine Jaeger, the landlady at the "Gasthof zum Falken", in Mainbernheim.

Stock:

6 juniper berries
2 bay leaves
6 peppercorns
1 pint wine vinegar
1 pint Silvaner wine (from Franconia)
1 pint water
½ tsp sugar
¼ tsp salt
2 onions
5 oz celeriac
3 carrots
8 oz leeks

4–6 pairs of coarse Franconian grilling sausages

Place the juniper berries, bay leaves and pepper in a loose leaf spice strainer, and make the stock using the ingredients listed above. Skin the onions and slice them into rings. Peel the celeriac and the carrots, wash the leeks. Cut the vegetables into very fine Julienne strips.
Bring the vegetables to the boil in the broth. Remove the pan from the heat and add the sausages. Put the pan back over a low heat and allow to simmer very gently for 20 minutes. Season with salt and pepper
Place one pair of sausages in deep soup dishes together with the vegetables and the stock, or serve everything together in a large soup terrine.

Kulmbach Beer-Knuckles

The number of beer breweries in Upper Franconia is particularly high. The Kulmbacher Beer Week takes place at the end of July and is one of the largest beer festivals in Germany.

4 pork fore knuckles
salt and pepper, freshly milled
6 juniper berries
2 onions, 1 garlic clove
4 oz clarified butter

2 pints meat stock
1 pint dark beer
1 tsp caraway powder
1 tsp crushed marjoram
¼ tsp thyme, dried
potato flour, to taste

Preheat the oven to 390°F.
Wash the knuckles under cold running water and dry with paper towels. Rub with salt, pepper and crushed juniper berries and then leave to stand for 30 minutes.
Peel the onions and garlic, and dice finely.
Heat the fat in a roasting pan and roast the meat with the onions and garlic on all sides. Deglaze with the stock and a little beer and add the remaining spices.
Leave the uncovered roasting pan in the oven for about two hours. Baste the meat several times with beer. If the crust starts to become too dark, cover the meat with aluminium foil.
Remove the roasted knuckles from the roasting pan and place them on warmed plates. Pour the sauce through a strainer – if necessary, add a little more stock. According to taste, the sauce can be served as it is, or bound with a light roux. If you want the sauce to be creamy, add a little potato flour mixed with cold water, and bring to the boil before serving.
Sauerkraut and potato dumplings (Silky Dumplings, see page 57) go well with this.

Hopfensprossensalat und Kümmerlesgmüs'
Hop Sprout Salad and Cooked Cucumber

Hopfensprossensalat

Hopfensprossen werden noch vor dem Spargel geerntet. Sie sind selbst während ihrer kurzen Saison (März/April) nicht einfach zu bekommen. Am ehesten noch dort in Franken, wo Hopfen angebaut wird, wie in Spalt, Hersbruck oder in der Hallertau, wo man die Sprossen frisch oder eingemacht bestellen kann.
Weil Hopfen, eine der wichtigsten Zutaten für die Bierherstellung, aber auch eine dekorative Pflanze ist, findet man sie inzwischen in privaten Gärten.

750 g Hopfensprossen
Salz, 2 l Wasser
2 Schalotten
1 TL Sonnenblumenöl
1 TL Walnussöl
1 EL Himbeeressig
1 TL Bier- oder Dijon-Senf
1 Prise Zucker, nach Geschmack
Pfeffer, frisch gemahlen

Hopfensprossen waschen und die holzigen Enden abschneiden.
Leicht gesalzenes Wasser in einem weiten Topf zum Kochen bringen und die Hopfensprossen darin ca. fünf Minuten sprudelnd kochen. Herd ausschalten und Sprossen noch fünf Minuten ziehen lassen.
Schalotten schälen und fein würfeln. Sonnenblumenöl in einem Topf erhitzen und die Schalottenwürfel einige Minuten darin anschwitzen. Schalottenwürfel in eine Schüssel geben, mit Walnussöl, Himbeeressig und Senf verrühren. Bei Verwendung von Senf ohne Zucker, noch eine Prise Zucker dazugeben.
Hopfensprossen abseihen. 150 ml des Kochsuds in die Schüssel gießen und mit den anderen Zutaten kräftig vermengen. Sprossen zuletzt unterheben, mit Salz und Pfeffer abschmecken. Vor dem Servieren noch mindestens eine Viertelstunde durchziehen lassen.

Kümmerlesgmüs' – Gurkengemüse

Eines der größten zusammenhängenden Gemüseanbaugebiete ist das Knoblauchsland, das sich zwischen Nürnberg, Fürth und Erlangen befindet. Die Region wurde bereits im achten Jahrhundert erschlossen und war in der Folge Nahrungslieferant für die Reichsstadt Nürnberg. Ihren Namen hat sie dem Umstand zu verdanken, dass dort früher anscheinend viel Zwiebeln angebaut wurden.

1 kg Gartengurken (Kümmerle)
2 Zwiebeln
2 Tomaten
50 g Butter
4 EL saure Sahne
4 EL Sahne/Rahm
2 TL Apfelessig
1 TL Paprikapulver
2 EL Dill, getrocknet
Salz und Pfeffer, frisch gemahlen

Gurken und Zwiebeln schälen. Zwiebeln fein hacken. Gurken halbieren. Kerne mit einem Löffel herausschaben. Gurken in zweifingerbreite Stücke schneiden.
Tomaten am Blütenansatz kreuzweise einschneiden und heiß überbrühen. In kaltes Wasser geben und die Haut abziehen. Tomaten vierteln, Strunk und Kerne entfernen.
Zwiebeln in der heißen Butter glasig anschwitzen. Tomaten und Gurken dazugeben, ca. zehn Minuten dünsten.
Saure und süße Sahne in einer kleinen Schüssel vermengen, mit Apfelessig, Paprikapulver, Dill sowie etwas Salz und Pfeffer vermischen. Sauce über das Gemüse geben und noch wenige Minuten köcheln lassen. Die Gurkenstücke dürfen noch einen gewissen Biss behalten.
Dieses Sommergemüse ist eine gute Beilage für viele Gerichte.

Hop Sprout Salad

Hop sprouts are not easy to come by even when they are in season. They are harvested before asparagus in a short period between March and April and can be found most easily in Franconia, since hops are grown in Spalt, Hersbruck and in Hallertau. There you can order the sprouts fresh, or in jars. Since hops are the most important ingredient for making beer, and because they're also decorative, these days you often find them in people's gardens.

10 oz hop sprouts
salt
4 pints water
2 shallots
1 tsp sunflower oil
1 tsp walnut oil
1 tbsp raspberry vinegar
1 tsp beer or Dijon mustard
1 pinch of sugar, to taste
pepper, freshly milled

Wash the hop sprouts and cut off the woody ends. Bring the lightly salted water to a rolling boil in a wide saucepan and boil the shoots for about five minutes. Turn off the heat and leave the sprouts to cook in the water for a further five minutes.
Peel the shallots and dice finely. Heat the sunflower oil in a pan and sweat the shallots for a few minutes.
Place the diced shallots in a bowl and mix them with the walnut oil, raspberry vinegar and mustard. If you use unsweetened mustard, add an extra pinch of sugar.
Drain the hop sprouts. Take one third pint of the cooking water and add it to the other ingredients, stirring thoroughly.
Finally, add the sprouts and season with salt and pepper.
Before serving, leave to marinate for at least 15 minutes.

Cooked Cucumber

One of the largest vegetable growing areas in the region is Knoblauchsland, or "garlic land", which lies between Nuremberg, Fürth and Erlangen. The land was cultivated as early as the 8th century, and in the following years it supplied food to the Free City of Nuremberg. The area owes its' name to the many onions that were apparently grown there in the past.

2 lb garden cucumbers
(so called "Kümmerle")
2 onions
2 tomatoes
2 oz butter
4 tbsp sour cream
4 tbsp fresh cream
2 tbsp cider vinegar
1 tsp paprika powder
2 tbsp dill, dried
salt and pepper, freshly milled

Peel the onions and the cucumbers. Finely chop the onions. Halve the cucumbers and scrape out the seeds with a spoon.
Cut the cucumbers into pieces approximately two fingers wide. Cut a cross into the tomatoes where the stalk was and pour hot water over them. Place the tomatoes in cold water and skin them. Cut them into quarters and remove the seeds.
Sweat the onions in butter until transparent. Add the tomatoes and cucumbers and fry gently for about ten minutes.
Mix the sour cream with the fresh cream in a small bowl and add the cider vinegar, paprika powder, dill and a little salt and pepper. Pour the sauce over the vegetables, and allow it to simmer for another few minutes. The cucumber should still be firm to the bite.
This summer vegetable dish is a suitable accompaniment to many dishes.

Lauwarmer Kartoffelsalat nach fränkischer Art

Der lauwarme Kartoffelsalat schmeckt zwar auch kalt, ist aber typisch und passt hervorragend zu Schnitzel oder gebackenem Leberkäse, zu Spiegeleiern oder gebratenem Fisch.
Das Rezept kann nach Lust und Laune mit Salat- oder Gewürzgurkenscheiben, Erbsen oder kleinen Karottenwürfeln variiert werden. In manchen Gegenden kommt noch 1 TL Senf in die Marinade.

2 kg Kartoffeln, vorwiegend festkochend
1 TL Kümmel
2 Lorbeerblätter
3 Zwiebeln
100 g durchwachsener Speck
Salz und Pfeffer, frisch gemahlen
½ l Gemüse- oder Fleischbrühe, erhitzt
3 EL neutrales Öl
3 EL Weinessig
2 EL frischer Schnittlauch, fein gehackt

Kartoffeln waschen. Mit der Schale in einen Topf mit Wasser geben. Zusammen mit Kümmel und Lorbeerblättern zum Kochen bringen. Hitze reduzieren und die Kartoffeln so lange kochen, bis sie gar, aber noch etwas bissfest sind (je nach Größe zwischen 15 und 30 Minuten). Kartoffeln abgießen und zum Ausdampfen beiseite stellen.
Zwiebeln schälen und klein würfeln. Speck ebenfalls in kleine Würfel schneiden. Speckwürfel in eine Pfanne geben und anbräunen lassen. Zwiebeln dazugeben und ca. zehn Minuten mitbraten. Kartoffeln schälen, in mittelfeine Scheiben schneiden (ca. 3 mm dick) und in eine Schüssel füllen. Speck und Zwiebeln dazugeben, salzen und pfeffern. Alles vorsichtig unterheben. Heiße Brühe mit Öl und Essig vermischen und die Hälfte darübergießen. Kartoffelsalat mindestens eine halbe Stunde ziehen lassen. Bevor er serviert wird, die restliche warme Marinade untermischen.
Vor dem Anrichten mit Schnittlauch überstreuen (Abbildung, Seite 25).

Halbseidene – Kartoffelklöße

Halbseidene Klöße (Seite 40) gehören zur vielfältigen Palette von Klößen aller Art, die man in Franken kennt. Als Beilage zu Braten- und Fleischgerichten werden sie geschätzt, aber auch zu Gemüse als vegetarisches Hauptgericht serviert. Im Nordosten Frankens mag man besonders grüne Klöße, die zu Zweidritteln aus rohen Kartoffeln und zu einem Drittel aus gekochten Kartoffeln bestehen.

2 kg mehlig kochende Kartoffeln
3 Milchbrötchen
3 EL Butter
$1/8$ l Milch
250 g Kartoffelmehl
Salz

Kartoffeln mit der Schale in einem großen Topf mit kaltem Wasser aufsetzen und zum Kochen bringen. Hitze etwas reduzieren und die Kartoffeln solange garen, bis die Schale aufzuplatzen beginnt. Abgießen und vollständig abkühlen lassen. Schälen und durch eine Kartoffelpresse drücken. Brötchen in kleinere Würfel schneiden. Butter in einer Pfanne erhitzen, Brötchenwürfel hineingeben und bei geringer Hitze goldbraun rösten. Dabei immer wieder wenden, damit sie nicht anbrennen.
Milch erhitzen. Kartoffelmehl zu den durchgepressten Kartoffeln geben, heiße Milch zugießen und alles gründlich vermengen. Leicht salzen und mit nassen Händen runde, tennisballgroße Klöße formen. In die Mitte von jedem Kloß ca.1 EL der vorbereiteten Croûtons füllen.
Leicht gesalzenes Wasser in einem großen Topf zum Kochen bringen. Etwas Kartoffelmehl ins Wasser geben, dann glänzen die Klöße beim Servieren schön. Nach und nach die Klöße in das sprudelnde Wasser gleiten lassen. Dann die Hitze reduzieren, damit die Klöße im leicht siedenden Wasser garen können. Sind sie alle nach oben gestiegen, noch zehn Minuten ziehen lassen.

Lukewarm Potato Salad, Franconian Style

This lukewarm potato salad also tastes good cold, but traditionally it's served lukewarm with breaded veal cutlet (Schnitzel), baked meatloaf, fried eggs or fried fish.
The recipe can be varied to include gherkins, peas or finely diced carrots. In some regions, a teaspoon of mustard is added to the marinade.

4 lb firm potatoes
1 tsp caraway
2 bay leaves
3 onions
4 oz streaky bacon
salt and pepper, freshly milled
1 pint vegetable of meat stock, heated
3 tbsp neutral tasting oil
3 tbsp wine vinegar
2 tbsp fresh chives, chopped finely

Wash the potatoes. Place them unpeeled in a pan with the water. Bring to the boil together with the caraway and the bay leaves, then reduce the heat and cook until the potatoes are done, but still have some bite (depending on how big they are, they'll need between 15 and 30 minutes). Drain the potatoes, place to one side, and allow the steam to evaporate.
Peel and dice the onions. Dice the bacon as well, and brown it in a pan. Add the onions, and fry together for a further ten minutes.
Peel the potatoes, and slice thinly (approx. an eighth of an inch). Place them in a bowl with the bacon and onions. Season with salt and pepper. Carefully fold the ingredients together. Mix the hot stock with the oil and vinegar and pour half of the liquid over the potatoes. Leave to stand for at least 30 minutes.
Before serving, carefully fold in the rest of the warm marinade and garnish with chives (picture see page 25).

Silky Potato Dumplings

Silky dumplings (page 40) are just one of the many types of dumplings that can be found in Franken. They are popular as a side dish served with roasts and other meat dishes, but also with vegetables as a vegetarian main course. In the north east of Franconia, "green dumplings" are particularly popular. These are made using two thirds raw potatoes, and one third cooked potatoes.

4 lb floury potatoes
3 white bread rolls
3 tbsp butter
¼ pint milk
9 oz potato flour
salt

Place the potatoes in a saucepan with cold water and bring to the boil. Reduce the heat a little, and cook the potatoes until the skins begin to burst. Drain and leave to cool completely. Peel the potatoes and mash them using either a potato masher or a press.
Cut the bread roll into cubes. Heat the butter in a frying pan. Add the bread cubes and fry them gently until they are golden brown, stirring regularly so that they don't burn.
Heat the milk. Add the potato flour to the mashed potatoes, pour in the hot milk and mix thoroughly. Add a little salt, and with wet hands, form round tennis ball sized dumplings. Fill each of the dumplings with approx. one tablespoon of the bread croutons.
Bring the lightly salted water to the boil in a large saucepan. If you add little potato flour to the water, the dumplings will have a shiny surface texture when you serve them. One by one, slide the dumplings gently into the water. Reduce the heat so that the dumplings can cook in the gently simmering water. Once they have all floated to the surface, cook them for a further ten minutes.

Erpflkoung
Potato Cake with Raisins

Serviettkloß

Der Serviettkloß wird gerne bei Familienfeiern serviert. Eine schöne Idee ist es, den Kloßteig in eine Guglhupf- oder Auflaufform zu füllen und dann im heißen Wasserbad zuzubereiten.
Der Serviettkloß passt gut zu feinen Braten oder zu Geflügel aller Art.

14 Brötchen, möglichst vom Vortag
½ l Milch, erhitzt
2 Zwiebeln
2 EL Butter
8–10 Eier
2 EL getrocknete Petersilie
Mehl
Salz und Pfeffer, frisch gemahlen

1 großes Baumwoll-Küchentuch, mit heißem Wasser gekocht (ohne Waschmittel)

Brötchen grob würfeln oder in Scheiben schneiden. In eine Schüssel füllen, mit der heißen Milch übergießen und abgedeckt eine halbe Stunde ziehen lassen.
Zwiebeln schälen, fein hacken und in heißer Butter in einer Bratpfanne anschwitzen. Mit Eiern und Petersilie zur Brötchenmasse geben, gut durchkneten. Mit Salz und Pfeffer abschmecken. Wenn die Masse zu weich ist, etwas Mehl untermengen.
Kloßteig in ein großes Küchentuch (Serviette) geben und locker an den vier Zipfeln zusammenbinden. Einen hohen Topf mit leicht gesalzenem Wasser zum Kochen bringen. Küchentuch an einem hölzernen Kochlöffel befestigen, der über den Topf mit dem sprudelnden Wasser gelegt wird. Hitze reduzieren und den Kloß bei mittlerer Temperatur kochen lassen, bis er gar ist. Das dauert mindestens eine Stunde, kann aber auch länger dauern. Der Kloß ist fertig, wenn der Teig eine feste Konsistenz angenommen hat.
Kloß aus dem Tuch nehmen, in Scheiben schneiden und servieren (Seite 34).

Erpflkoung – Blechkuchen mit Kartoffeln und Rosinen

Eine Spezialität aus dem Hofer Land und dem angrenzenden sächsischen Vogtland, wo man besonders viele Rezepte mit Kartoffeln kennt. Erpfl kommt von dem in Süddeutschland häufig für Kartoffel genutzten Wort „Erdapfel".

300 g Kartoffeln
1/8 l Milch, 20 g Frischhefe
250 g Mehl, 120 g Zucker
1 Pck Vanillezucker
½ unbehandelte Bio-Zitrone, Schalenabrieb
1 Prise Salz, 2 Eier
150 g Butter, 80 g Rosinen
3 EL Zucker, mit etwas Zimtpulver vermischt

Kartoffeln in der Schale kochen und auskühlen lassen. Dann schälen und fein reiben.
Milch in einem Topf lauwarm auf Körpertemperatur erhitzen und vom Herd nehmen. Hefe hineinbröckeln und verrühren, bis sie sich aufgelöst hat. Mehl mit Zucker, Vanillezucker, Zitronenschalenabrieb und Salz in einer Schüssel vermischen.
100 g Butter sanft erhitzen, bis sie flüssig ist. Hefemilch in die Schüssel zur Mehlmischung gießen, flüssige Butter und Eier dazugeben. Teig so lange durcharbeiten, bis er geschmeidig ist. Geriebene Kartoffeln und Rosinen hinzufügen, alles gründlich durchkneten. Teig mit einem Tuch abdecken und an einem warmen, zugfreien Ort 45 Minuten gehen lassen. Backofen auf 180 °C vorheizen.
Backblech buttern, Teig gleichmäßig mit einem Messer aufstreichen und nochmals ca. zehn Minuten gehen lassen. Anschließend mit einer Gabel Löcher in die Teigoberfläche stechen. Blech auf der mittleren Schiene im vorgeheizten Ofen 20–30 Minuten backen. Der Kuchen ist fertig, wenn seine Oberfläche leicht golden ist.
Kuchen aus dem Ofen nehmen und etwas abkühlen lassen. Noch warm mit der restlichen, flüssigen Butter bestreichen und mit Zimtzucker gleichmäßig überstreuen.

Napkin Dumpling

Napkin Dumplings are often served at family celebrations. A nice idea is to fill the dumpling mix into a traditional guglhupf form, or soufflé mould, and cook it in a bain marie. This dumpling is good served with fine roasts and all types of poultry.

14 bread rolls, if possible a day old
1 pint milk, heated
2 onions
2 tbsp butter
8–10 eggs
2 tbsp dried parsley
flour
salt and pepper, freshly milled

1 large cotton tea towel, or napkin, boiled in hot water (without detergent)

Dice the bread rolls, or cut them into slices and place them in a bowl. Pour in the hot milk, cover and leave to stand for half an hour.
Peel the onions, chop finely and sweat with butter in a frying pan. Add to the bread mixture along with the eggs and parsley, then knead thoroughly. Season with salt and pepper.
If the mixture is too soft, stir in some flour.
Place the dough on a large tea towel (or napkin) and tie the four corners together.
Bring a tall pan of lightly salted water to the boil. Slide a wooden cooking spoon sideways through the knot in the tea towel, and lower the dumpling into the water so that the spoon rests on the edges of the saucepan – this stops the dumpling from touching the base of the saucepan and burning. Reduce the heat and cook the dumpling at medium heat until it is done. This will take at least one hour, but maybe longer. The dumpling is ready when the dough is firm to the touch.
Remove the dumpling from the tea towel, slice, and serve (page 34).

Erpflkoung – Potato Cake with Raisins

These are a speciality from Hofer Land and neighbouring Vogtland, in Saxony, where you can find a lot of potato recipes. The word "Erpfl" comes from "Erdapfel" or "earth apples", as potatoes are frequently called in southern Germany.

300 g potatoes
¼ pint milk, ¾ oz fresh yeast
9 oz flour, 4 oz sugar
1 packet of vanilla sugar (approx. ¼ oz)
peel of ½ unwaxed lemon
1 pinch of salt, 2 eggs
5 oz butter, 3 oz raisins
3 tbsp sugar mixed with cinnamon

Cook the potatoes in their skins and allow them to cool. Peel and then grate finely.
Warm the milk in a saucepan until it is lukewarm, then remove it from the heat. Crumble in the fresh yeast and stir until it has dissolved.
Mix the flour, sugar, vanilla sugar, lemon peel and salt in a bowl.
Gently melt 4 oz butter.
Pour the yeast mixture into the flour, then add the melted butter and the eggs. Knead the dough until it is smooth. Add the grated potatoes and the raisins and knead thoroughly again. Cover the dough with a cloth and leave to rise in a warm, draft free place for 45 minutes.
Preheat the oven to 355°F.
Grease the baking tray with butter, and spread out the dough using a knife. Leave to rise again for about ten minutes.
Prick the surface of the dough all over with a fork. Place the baking tray in the middle of the preheated oven and bake for 20–30 minutes. The cake is done when the surface is a light golden brown color.
Remove the cake from the oven and leave to cool for a while. Using a pastry brush, paint the cake with the rest of the melted butter, then sprinkle with cinnamon sugar.

Kniekiechla · Knee Cakes

Kniekiechla

Schmalzgebäck hat eine lange Tradition in Franken. Früher wurde es in erster Linie bei wichtigen Familienfeiern oder Kirchweihfesten angeboten. Nicht nur im Hofer und Bayreuther Land gab es richtige Kiechlabäckerinnen, die ins Haus kamen, um die wohlschmeckenden Gebäckstücke direkt vor Ort zu backen. Heute werden die Kiechla in guten Bäckereien angeboten.
Überliefert ist, dass ihr oberfränkischer Name Kniekiechla daher kommt, dass so manche Kiechlabäckerin den Teig über ihr Knie gelegt hat, um ihn schön groß und rund auszuziehen. Daher wird das Gebäck auch als „Ausgezogene" bezeichnet

- ¼ l Milch
- 30 g Frischhefe
- 500 g Weizenmehl, Type 405
- 1 Prise Salz
- 5 EL Zucker
- 2 Eier
- 1 TL Schalenabrieb von einer unbehandelten Bio-Zitrone
- 3 EL Öl

Butterschmalz zum Frittieren
Puderzucker

Milch lauwarm erhitzen. Hefe hineinbröckeln und verrühren. Mehl mit Salz und Zucker in einer Schüssel gründlich vermischen. Eine Vertiefung in die Mitte drücken und die Hefemilch hineingießen. An der Seite Eier, Zitronenschalenabrieb und Öl dazugeben und von dort aus alles vorsichtig vermengen. Dann den Teig durchkneten, bis er glänzt, Blasen wirft und sich von der Schüssel löst. Alles mit einem Tuch abdecken und an einem warmen, zugfreien Ort gehen lassen.
Hat sich das Teigvolumen sichtlich vergrößert, den Teig nochmals durchkneten und weitere zehn Minuten ruhen lassen.
Zum Formen auf eine mit Mehl bestäubte Unterlage legen, dünn auswellen (ca. ½ cm dick) und mit einem Glas Rondellen ausstechen (Durchmesser ca. 7 cm). Diese wieder mit einem Tuch abdecken und nochmals fünf Minuten gehen lassen. Kiechla mit den Händen so drehen und ausziehen, dass in der Mitte ein dünnes, fast durchsichtiges Fenster entsteht.
Butterschmalz in einer geräumigen Edelstahlform auf 180 °C erhitzen. Jedes Gebäckstück nach und nach im sprudelnden Schmalz schwimmend goldbraun ausbacken. Zum Auskühlen auf ein mit Küchenkrepp belegtes Holzbrett legen, später mit Puderzucker bestreuen.

Kniekiechla – Knee Cakes

Pastries have a long tradition in Franconia. In the past they used to be served at important family celebrations or religious festivals. Throughout the region, but particularly in Hofer and the region around Bayreuth, female pastry bakers would come to your house and prepare the pastries right in your own kitchen. These days, the pastries are prepared in most good bakeries. According to legend, the term "Kniekiechla" comes from the German word for knee, "Knie". Tradition has it that some of the baker women would put the dough on their knees so that they could pull the pastries into shape, since the cakes had to be big and round, and very thin in the middle. That's also the reason they call this type of pastry "Ausgezogene", or "stretched pastries".

½ pint milk
1 cube of fresh yeast (approx. 2 oz)
1 lb plain flour
1 pinch of salt
5 tbsp sugar
2 eggs
peel of 1 unwaxed lemon
3 tbsp oil
clarified butter for frying
powdered sugar

Heat the milk until it is lukewarm. Crumble the fresh yeast into the milk.
Mix the flour, salt and sugar thoroughly in a bowl. Form a well in the heap of flour, and pour in the yeast mixture. From the side of the bowl, add the eggs, lemon peel and oil, and mix carefully. Knead the dough until it becomes glossy and begins to form air bubbles. At this stage, it should come away from the side of the bowl easily. Cover with a cloth and leave to rise in a warm, draft free place.
Once the dough has increased considerably in size, knead it through once again and leave to rise for another ten minutes.
Sprinkle the work surface with flour and stretch the dough (or use a rolling pin) until it is about one quarter of an inch thick. Using a glass, cut out circles that are approx. two inches wide. Cover them with a cloth and leave them to rise again for five minutes.
Using your hands, stretch the "Kiechla", so that an almost transparent window forms in the centre of the circle.
Heat the clarified butter in a wide stainless steel pan to 355°F. Fry the pastries one by one in the bubbling fat until they float on the surface and are a golden brown color. Leave to cool on wooden board covered with paper towel and later dust them with powdered sugar.

Zwetschgerblootz mit Streuseln

Der Blootz ist ein Hefekuchen, den es sowohl in herzhaften als auch in süßen Varianten gibt. Sein mundartlicher Name ist von „Platz" abgeleitet, denn früher wurden diese Kuchen am Backtag nebenher im Ofen gebacken, wo eben noch Platz war.
Im oberfränkischen Obstanbaugebiet in der Fränkischen Schweiz ist die Fränkische Hauszwetschge vorherrschend. Sie wird außer zum Backen und für Kompott gerne für die hervorragende Obstbrände dieser Gegend verwendet.
Frisch aus dem Ofen schmeckt so ein Blootz mit Zwetschgen einfach köstlich. Er lässt sich aber auch gut einfrieren.

Teig:

500 g Mehl
70 g Zucker
½ l Milch, erwärmt
43 g Frischhefe (1 Würfel)
100 g Butterschmalz, erwärmt, bis es sich verflüssigt
1 großes Ei
1 Prise Salz

Belag:

2½ kg Zwetschgen
350 g Mehl
200 g Zucker
1 Pck Vanillezucker
200 g Butter

Mehl in eine hohe Schüssel sieben, mit dem Zucker vermengen und eine Mulde hineindrücken. Erwärmte Milch mit der darin aufgelösten Hefe in die Mulde gießen und mit etwas Mehl vom Muldenrand zu einem Vorteig verrühren. Schüssel mit einem Tuch abdecken und 15 Minuten an einem warmen, zugfreien Ort gehen lassen.
Butterschmalz zum Vorteig gießen, Ei und Salz dazugeben. Alles gründlich vermengen, bis der Teig Blasen wirft. Wieder abdecken und nochmals 15 Minuten gehen lassen.
Währenddessen die Zwetschgen vorbereiten: waschen, einschneiden und Stein entfernen.
Für die Streusel Mehl in eine Schüssel sieben, mit Zucker und Vanillezucker vermischen. Butter in einem Töpfchen zerlassen und warm halten.
Backofen auf 220 °C vorheizen.
Ein Backblech mit etwas Butter ausstreichen. Teig mit Mehlhilfe gleichmäßig ausrollen und das Blech damit belegen. Zwetschgen mit der geschlossenen Seite dicht auf den Teig legen. Blootz auf der mittleren Schiene im Backofen ca. 30 Minuten backen.
Warme Butter über die Mehl-Zucker-Mischung träufeln und mit einer Gabel so vermengen, dass sich Streusel bilden. Nach der halben Backzeit auf dem fertigen Blootz verteilen.

Damson Cake with Crumble Topping

"Blootz" is a yeast cake that you can get in sweet and savoury form. The name comes from the German word for space, "Platz". In the past, "Blootz" was cooked on baking day whenever there was some space for it in the oven.
In Franconian Switzerland, the main fruit farming area in the region, Franconian Damask plums are grown extensively. Apart from their use in the kitchen, for cakes and compotes, they are widely used for making the region's excellent fruit brandies.
When it comes fresh from the oven, this plum cake tastes simply delicious. And it freezes well if you want to eat on another day.

Dough:

1 lb flour
2 ½ oz sugar
1 pint milk, heated
1 cube of fresh yeast (approx. 2 oz)
4 oz clarified butter, melted
1 large egg
1 pinch of salt

Topping:

10 lb damsons
12 oz flour
8 oz sugar
1 packet of vanilla sugar (approx. ¼ oz)
8 oz butter

Sieve the flour into a deep bowl, mix with the sugar and make a well in the flour. Pour the warm milk with the dissolved yeast into the well and mix in some of the flour from the sides of the well to make the initial dough. Cover the bowl with a cloth and leave in a warm, draft free place for 15 minutes.
Pour the melted, clarified butter into the bowl and add the egg and salt. Mix everything thoroughly, until the dough begins to form air bubbles. Cover again and leave to rise for another 15 minutes.
In the meantime, prepare the damsons: wash, make a small incision, and remove the stones.
For the crumble, sieve the flour into a bowl, mix in the sugar and vanilla sugar. Melt the butter and keep it warm.
Preheat the oven to 430°F.
Grease the baking tray with butter. Using some flour to roll out the dough so that it covers the tray evenly. Place the damsons close together on the dough with the incision facing upwards.
Bake on the middle shelf of the oven for about 30 minutes.

Kirschmännla · Cherry Bread Pudding

Kirschmännla

In der Fränkischen Schweiz liebt man Rezepte mit Süßkirschen, die dort gut gedeihen. Die Region ist für ihre Kirschbäume berühmt, denn das milde Klima ist für das größte zusammenhängende Kirschanbaugebiet Europas verantwortlich. Jedes Jahr im Juli findet in Pretzfeld im Kellerwald das Fränkische Kirschenfest statt.
Das Traditionsrezept stammt von der Nürnberger Confiserie Neef, die auch regionale Familienrezepte pflegt. Am besten schmeckt diese echt fränkische Spezialität, wenn das Kirschmännla warm mit kalter Vanillesauce serviert wird!

Kirschmännla:

10 Brötchen vom Vortag (Milch- oder Wasserbrötchen)
½ l Milch
½ l Sahne/Rahm
4 Eier
100 g Zucker
½ unbehandelt Bio-Zitrone, Schalenabrieb
2 TL Zimtpulver
1,8 kg frische Kirschen (Süß- oder Sauerkirschen)
120 g Butter

Vanillesauce:

¼ l Milch
¼ l Sahne/Rahm
3 Eigelbe
40 g Zucker
10 g Speisestärke
1 Vanillestange, ausgekratztes Mark

Alte Brötchen in Würfel schneiden.
Milch, Sahne, Eier, die Hälfte des Zuckers und Zitronenschalenabrieb in einer Schüssel mit dem elektrischen Handrührgerät glattrühren.
Backofen auf 180 °C vorheizen.
Frische Kirschen entsteinen. Brötchen, Kirschen und die Hälfte des Zimts unter die Eier-Sahne-Mischung heben und etwas ziehen lassen. Den restlichen Zucker und Zimt vermischen und beiseite stellen.
Backblech oder ofenfeste Form (ca. 30 × 15 cm, 5–6 cm hoch) kräftig ausbuttern und die Masse einfüllen. Auf der mittleren Schiene in den vorgeheizten Backofen schieben. Nach einer halben Stunde mit flüssiger Butter bepinseln, Zimtzucker darüberstreuen. Dann noch ca. 20 Minuten fertigbacken.
In der Zwischenzeit die Vanillesauce zubereiten. Dazu Milch, Sahne, Eigelbe, Zucker, Speisestärke und Vanillemark unter ständigem Rühren im Wasserbad aufschlagen, bis die Masse sämig ist. Abkühlen lassen und separat zum Kirschmännla reichen.

Cherry Bread Pudding

Sweet cherries grow well in Franconian Switzerland, and the recipes that use them are very popular. The region is famous for its cherry trees, because the mild climate has resulted in the largest cherry farming area in Europe. Every July, the annual Franconian cherry festival is held in the town of Pretzfeld, in the Kellerwald.
This traditional recipe comes from Confiserie Neef, in Nuremberg, who use many regional family recipes. This Franconian speciality tastes best when served warm with cold vanilla sauce!

10 one day old bread rolls (white bread)
1 pint milk
1 pint cream
4 eggs
4 oz sugar
½ unwaxed lemon (peel)
2 tsp cinnamon power
3 lb 15 oz fresh cherries (sweet or black cherries)
4½ oz butter

Vanilla sauce:

½ pint milk
½ pint cream
3 egg yolks
1½ oz sugar
⅓ oz cornflour
1 vanilla pod

Cut the bread rolls into small cubes. Using an electric whisk, mix the milk, cream, eggs, half of the sugar, and the lemon peel in a bowl. Preheat the oven to 355°F.
Pit the cherries. Fold the bread, cherries and half of the cinnamon into the egg and cream mixture and leave to stand for a while. Mix the remaining sugar with the rest of the cinnamon and put aside. Grease a baking tray, or baking dish, generously with butter. Pour in the batter and place on the middle shelf of the preheated oven. After half an hour, baste with melted butter and sprinkle with the cinnamon sugar. Bake for a further 20 minutes.
In the meantime, prepare the vanilla sauce.
Whisk the milk, cream, egg yolk, sugar, corn flour and vanilla seeds over a bain marie until it has a creamy consistency.
Leave to cool and serve separately in a jug together with the Cherry Bread Pudding.

Schwarz Maadla
Franconian Blueberry Tiramisu

Schwarz Maadla – fränkisches Heidelbeer-Tiramisù

In den ausgedehnten Wäldern des Fichtelgebirges und Frankenwalds wachsen die niedrigen Sträucher der Schwarzbeeren, wie sie dort genannt werden, besonders gut. Von altersher wurden die saftigen kleinen Beeren im Sommer gesammelt und für süße Speisen verwendet. Das Familienrezept Schwarz Maadla (fränkisch für „schwarzes Mädchen") ist eine leckere Nachspeise für besondere Anlässe.

Biskuitteig:

4 Eier, getrennt
3 EL Wasser, handwarm
150 g Zucker
1 Pck Vanillezucker
70 g Mehl
1 Prise Salz
70 g Speisestärke
½ TL Backpulver

1 hohe Springform, Ø 26 cm

Füllung:

50 g Zucker
1 kg Heidelbeeren (Schwarzbeeren), küchenfertig
4 EL Heidelbeer-Konfitüre
6 EL Haselnüsse, geröstet und fein gehackt
2 EL Rum oder Obstler
700 ml Sahne/Rahm
Schokoraspel oder -späne aus dunkler Kuvertüre

Für den Biskuit Eigelbe, Wasser, Zucker und Vanillezucker in eine Schüssel geben und auf höchster Stufe mit dem elektrischen Handrührgerät schaumig hellgelb rühren. Mehl in einer separaten Schüssel mit Salz, Stärke und Backpulver mischen. Nach und nach über die Eigelbmasse sieben und untermengen. Eiweiß steif schlagen und unterheben. Backofen auf 180 °C vorheizen.
Eine Springform mit Backpapier auslegen. Teig hineinfüllen, mit einem Messer glattstreichen und ca. 30 Minuten auf der mittleren Schiene backen, bis seine Oberfläche golden gebräunt ist. Backofen ausschalten und den Biskuit noch ein paar Minuten darin stehen lassen. Dann herausnehmen und vollständig auskühlen lassen. Zwei Mal quer durchschneiden, sodass drei dünne Böden entstehen.
Für die Füllung Zucker in einer hohen Pfanne goldgelb karamellisieren und glattrühren. Die Hälfte der Heidelbeeren auf ein Blech geben und mit dem heißen Karamell zügig übergießen. Heidelbeer-Konfitüre in einer kleinen Schüssel mit Rum oder Obstler vermischen. Sahne mit etwas Zucker sehr steif schlagen.
Eine hohe, breite Glasschale mit dem ersten Biskuitboden auslegen verteilen. Zwei Drittel der Krokant-Heidelbeeren mit etwas frischen Heidelbeeren gleichmäßig darauf platzieren und einen Teil der Schlagsahne darauf verteilen. Zweiten Biskuit auflegen, mit Haselnüssen bestreuen und mit etwas Sahne bestreichen. Letzten Biskuit auflegen, Heidelbeer-Konfitüre aufstreichen, mit den restlichen rohen und karamellisierten Heidelbeeren belegen und dekorativ über die gesamte Fläche Tupfer der restlichen Schlagsahne verteilen. Oder die Nachspeise auf einzelne Serviergläser verteilen und darin einschichten.
Schüssel oder Portionsgläser drei Stunden in den Kühlschrank stellen und vor dem Servieren mit Schokoraspeln oder -spänen bestreuen.

Franconian Blueberry Tiramisu

In the expansive forests of the Fichtelgebirge and Frankenwald, the low blueberry bushes grow particularly well. Locally, they are called "Schwarzbeeren", which translates in English as, "black berries". But don't let that confuse you into thinking they really are referring to what we call blackberries in English, since they are called "Brombeeren" in German! As long as anyone can recall, the juicy little berries have always been collected in summer and used for desserts. This family recipe "Schwarz Maadla", (which is Franconian for "dark haired girls"), is a delicious dessert on special occasions.

Sponge:

4 eggs, separated
3 tbsp water, lukewarm
5 oz sugar
1 packet of vanillar sugar (approx. ¼ oz)
2 ½ oz flour
1 pinch of salt
2 ½ oz cornflour
½ tsp baking powder

1 round spring form baking tin, Ø 10 inches

Filling:

4 eggs
1 ½ oz sugar
2 lb blueberries (huckleberries), cleaned
4 tbsp blueberry jam
6 tbsp hazelnuts, roasted and finely chopped
2 tbsp rum or fruit brandy
1 ½ pints cream
grated dark chocolate

For the sponge: Place the egg yolks, water, sugar and vanilla sugar in a bowl. Using an electric whisk, mix at the highest speed, until the mixture is fluffy and light yellow.
In a separate bowl, sieve the flour salt, corn flour and baking powder. Add the flour to the whisked egg yolk a bit at a time, and fold it in carefully.
Whisk the egg whites until stiff and fold into the mixture.
Preheat the oven to 355°F.
Line a spring form baking tin with greaseproof paper. Pour in the cake mixture and use a knife to spread it evenly. Bake for 30 minutes on the middle shelf of the oven until the surface is golden brown. Turn off the oven and leave the cake in the oven for a few minutes. Then take it out and leave it to cool completely. Cut the sponge horizontally into three slices.
For the filling, caramelize the sugar in a deep saucepan and stir until smooth. Place half of the blueberries on a baking tray and quickly pour the caramel over them.
In a small bowl, mix the blueberry jam with the rum or fruit brandy. Beat the cream with a little sugar until it is very stiff.
Take a deep, wide glass serving dish, and add the bottom sponge layer. Place two thirds of the caramel blueberries together with a few fresh blueberries over the sponge, and then cover with some of the cream. Place the second sponge layer on top, sprinkle with the hazelnuts and cover with some more cream. Then add the last sponge layer and spread it with the blueberry jam. Place the remaining caramel blueberries and fresh berries on the top layer of the sponge, and spoon the remaining dollops of cream over the dish.
If you prefer, you can make individual serving portions instead of one big bowl.
Leave to cool in the refrigerator for three hours and, before serving, decorate with the grated chocolate.

Nürnberger Elisenlebkuchen
Nuremberg Elisen Gingerbread

Nürnberger Elisenlebkuchen

Nürnberger Lebkuchen sind weltweit bekannt und zu einem Synonym für Weihnachtsgebäck geworden. Ihre Geschichte lässt sich bis ins 15. Jahrhundert zurückverfolgen. Anno 1487 ließ Kaiser Friedrich III. anlässlich eines Reichstags die Kinder der Stadt in den Burggraben kommen und kleine Lebkuchen mit seinem Konterfei verteilen. Das wurde mit großer Begeisterung aufgenommen. Nürnberg war im Mittelalter Handelszentrum für exotische Gewürze und im nahen Nürnberger Reichswald gab es viele Imker – ideal für die Lebkuchenproduktion. Auch heute backen viele fränkische Bäckereien und Konditoreien in der Adventszeit eigene Lebkuchen.
Dieses Rezept stammt von der Confiserie Neef aus Nürnberg, in der noch heute handwerklich hochwertige Lebkuchen in allen Variationen hergestellt werden.

300 g Haselnüsse
12 Eiweiß
700 g Zucker
240 g Marzipanrohmasse
120 g Zitronat, gewürfelt
120 g Orangeat, gewürfelt
300 g Mandeln, fein gerieben
180 g Weizenmehl, Type 405
30 g Lebkuchengewürz*
15 g Hirschhornsalz**

40 runde Oblaten, Ø 10cm

Glasur:

150 g Puderzucker
100 g dunkle Kuvertüre

Garnitur:

halbierte Mandeln
kandierte Zitronatscheiben

Haselnüsse auf einem Backblech im Ofen bei ca. 170 °C rösten. Häutchen durch Rubbeln entfernen, Nüsse grob reiben.
Eiweiß und Zucker zu steifem Eischnee schlagen. Mehl, Marzipanrohmasse, Zitronat, Orangeat, Haselnüsse, Mandelmehl, Lebkuchengewürz und Hirschhornsalz in eine Schüssel geben. Mit dem Knethaken einer Küchenmaschine unter langsamer Zugabe des Eischnees kräftig durcharbeiten und glattrühren.
Je 60g dieser Masse abwiegen und so auf runde Oblaten streichen, dass sie in der Mitte etwas dicker sind. Masse mithilfe eines Spatels zum Rand hin flach ausstreichen. Dazu jede Oblate vorher am besten auf ein rundes Unterteil mit demselben Durchmesser legen, zum Beispiel den Boden eines Glases. Das erleichtert die Arbeit.
Lebkuchen auf ein Backblech legen. Die Hälfte der Lebkuchen mit bis zu fünf Mandelhälften und einem kleinen, dünnen Stück kandierter Zitronenscheibe dekorieren. Die andere Hälfte der Lebkuchen unbelegt lassen.
Blech über Nacht offen in der Küche stehen lassen, damit die Lebkuchen abtrocknen können.
Am nächsten Morgen den Backofen auf 190°C vorheizen.
Backblech auf der mittleren Schiene in den Ofen schieben, Lebkuchen darin 12–13 Minuten backen.
Belegte Lebkuchen noch in heißem Zustand glasieren: Puderzucker dazu mit etwas Wasser anrühren und die Lebkuchen dünn bepinseln.
Unbelegte Lebkuchen ganz auskühlen lassen. Kuvertüre in einem Wasserbadtopf erhitzen, bis sie flüssig ist, und die Lebkuchen damit bestreichen.

* Fertiges Lebkuchengewürz enthält meist Zimt, Orangenschalen, Koriander, Zitronenschalen, Sternanis, Fenchelsamen, Muskatblüte, Nelken und Kardamon.

** Backtriebmittel, das vor allem für weihnachtliches Gebäck verwendet wird. Ursprünglich wurde es tatsächlich aus Geweihen von Hirschen hergestellt.

Nuremberg Elisen Gingerbread

Nuremberg's gingerbread is famous throughout the world and has become synonymous with Christmas cookies. Its history dates back to the 15th century. In 1487, on the occasion of the Reichstag (a meeting of the Imperial Legislature), Emperor Frederick III. had the city's children stand in the castle moat and hand out small gingerbread cookies with his portrait on them. They were received with great enthusiasm.

In the Middle Ages, Nuremberg was a trade centre for exotic spices, and in the nearby forests of the Nuremberg Reichswald there were many bee keepers – ideal conditions for producing gingerbread. To this day, many Franconian bakeries produce their own gingerbread during advent.

This recipe comes from Confiserie Neef, where they still produce a wide variety of high quality, handmade gingerbread in Nuremberg.

10 ½ oz hazelnuts
12 egg whites
1 lb 9 oz sugar
8 ½ oz marzipan / almond paste
4 oz candied lemon peel, diced
4 oz candied orange peel, diced
10 ½ oz finely ground almonds
6 oz plain flour
1 oz gingerbread spice*
½ oz ammonium carbonate (salt of the hartshorn)**
40 round baking wafers, Ø 10cm

Glaze:

50 oz powdered sugar
4 oz dark cooking chocolate

To decorate:

halved almonds
candied lemon peel

Roast the hazelnuts in the oven at 340°F, for about 15 minutes. Remove the skins by rubbing them and then grate them roughly.

Whisk the egg whites and the sugar until the mixture forms stiff peaks.

Place the flour, marzipan, candied lemon and orange peel, hazelnuts, ground almonds, gingerbread spice and ammonium carbonate in a bowl. Using the dough hook on your kitchen mixer knead the ingredients thoroughly, and slowly add the whisked egg whites until the mixture is smooth. Place two oz portions of the dough on each of the round cooking wafers so that the mixture is a little thicker in the middle than at the sides. This is much easier if you first place the baking wafer on an upturned water glass. Using a pallet knife, spread the dough evenly, then place the gingerbread on a baking tray. Decorate half of the cookies with up to five almonds and a thin piece of candied lemon peel. Leave the others undecorated. Leave the baking tray to stand in the kitchen overnight so that the gingerbread can dry out.

The next morning, preheat the oven to 375°F. Place the baking tray in the middle of the preheated oven and bake the gingerbread for 12–15 minutes.

While the decorated gingerbread is still hot, add a little water to the icing sugar and paint a thin glaze over the cookies.

Once the undecorated gingerbread cookies have cooled completely, melt the cooking chocolate in a bain marie, and use it to paint the cookies.

* Pre-packed gingerbread spice usually contains cinnamon, orange peel, coriander, lemon peel, star aniseed, fennel seed, mace, cloves and cardamom.

** A type of baking power that is used primarily for specific kinds of baked goods at Christmas. (In the past it really was made from stag horns!)

1

2

3

7

8

10

11

12

Frankens viele Gesichter
The many faces of Franconia

Franken ist nicht leicht zu fassen. Das Land hat viele Gesichter, und seine Ränder sind unscharf. In Franken konnte sich, soweit wir auch zurückschauen, eine einheitliche Staatsgewalt nicht ausbilden. Ein Nebeneinander mehrerer großer und vieler kleiner Herrschaftsgebilde machte das Land bunt und vielgestaltig. So gab es katholische neben evangelischen Landstrichen, dazu – ungleich übers Land verteilt – viele Judengemeinden. Manche Bereiche waren früh und stark industriell geprägt, während andere Gegenden bis weit ins 20. Jahrhundert ihr landwirtschaftliches Gesicht bewahrten.

Franken hatte keine klaren Grenzen. Was man unter dem Namen „Franken" verstand, war im Mittelalter einem starken Wandel unterworfen: Das Herzogtum Franken, das im frühen 10. Jahrhundert zu entstehen begann, aber über Ansätze nie hinauskam, griff weit aus: im Westen bis über Worms und Speyer hinaus, im Norden bis in den Raum Kassel. Im Spätmittelalter war der Landstrich, den man als Franken bezeichnete, sehr klein geworden: Wer vom „Land zu Franken" sprach, der meinte den Raum zwischen Steigerwald und Spessart, das Kernland des Hochstifts Würzburg.

Erst der 1500 ins Leben gerufene Fränkische Reichskreis gab Franken Halt und Bestand und stiftete fränkische Identität. Er vereinte die Fürstbistümer Bamberg, Würzburg und Eichstätt, die Markgraftümer Ansbach und Kulmbach-Bayreuth, die Herrschaften des Deutschen Ordens um Mergentheim und Ellingen, die Reichsstädte Nürnberg, Rothenburg, Schweinfurt, Weißenburg und Windsheim, dazu eine Reihe von Grafen und Herren: Henneberg, Hohenlohe, Wertheim, Castell, Rieneck, Schwarzenberg, Schenk von Limpurg, Schenk von Erbach. Dieses Franken erstreckte sich von der böhmischen Grenze bis in den Odenwald, vom heute thüringischen Salzungen bis Eichstätt. Der Reichskreis griff einerseits weiter aus als der fränkische Sprachraum – im Fichtelgebirge reden die Eingesessenen bis heute Nordbairisch –, andererseits zählten die sächsischen Herzogtümer südlich des Thüringer Waldes, wo die Menschen einen fränkischen Zungenschlag hatten, nicht zum Fränkischen Reichskreis.

Franken war kleingliedrig. Es gab neben den Grafschaften, Reichsstädten und Fürstentümern noch Hunderte ritterschaftlicher Orte. Da die Ritter im 16. Jahrhundert die Reichsunmittelbarkeit erlangten, waren die Niederadligen und ihre Dörfer nicht einem nahen Fürsten, sondern ausschließlich dem fernen Kaiser untertan.

Das vielgesichtige Franken, geprägt durch ständige Reibereien im Kleinen, wurde im frühen 19. Jahrhundert ausgelöscht. Nachdem sich 1792 das Königreich Preußen die Fürstentümer Ansbach und Bayreuth angegliedert hatte, verleibte sich ab 1802 Bayern einen großen Teil Frankens ein: zuerst die geistlichen Staaten und die meisten Reichsstädte, 1806 dann Ansbach, Nürnberg und die vielen Adelsdörfer, 1810 Bayreuth. Würzburg ging Bayern 1805 verloren, wurde aber 1814 wiedererlangt. Andere Teile Frankens – das Land an Jagst und Tauber oder der Odenwald – gelangten im frühen 19. Jahrhundert an Hessen, Baden und Württemberg.

Das Bayern jener Zeit sollte ein Einheitsstaat sein. Es war verpönt, von Franken zu sprechen. Bayern wurde 1808 in Kreise (heute Regierungsbezirke) gegliedert, die, französischem Vorbild folgend, nach Flüssen benannt waren. Historische Gegebenheiten spielten keine Rolle.

Erst bei der Neugliederung Bayerns im Jahr 1837 wurden die alten „Stammes"grenzen wieder berücksichtigt, und die neuen Namen verwiesen auf die Geschichte: „Oberfranken", „Mittelfranken" und „Unterfranken und Aschaffenburg" – letzterer Ort wurde historisch akkurat genannt, weil der Untermain um die kurmainzische Residenzstadt Aschaffenburg in der Neuzeit nicht als fränkisch gegolten hatte. Durch die Verbindung mit Unterfranken wurde aber auch diese Gegend fränkisch.

Prof. Dr. Günter Dippold,
Bezirksheimatpfleger und Kulturreferent
des Bezirks Oberfranken und Honorarprofessor
an der Otto-Friedrich-Universität Bamberg

Franconia is hard to define. The state has many faces and its boundaries are unclear. No matter how far back you go, it was never possible to form a unified federal state here. Several large governing structures coexisted alongside numerous smaller ones, and a patchwork landscape of Catholic and Protestant areas along with many unevenly distributed Jewish communities resulted in a diverse and colourful state. Some areas were strongly industrialized quite early on, whereas others maintained their rural character well into the 20th century.

Franconia had no clear borders. During the Middle Ages what was understood to be "Franconia" changed considerably. The Duchy of Franconia, which began to form in the early 10th century, extended quite a distance: in the West, it stretched beyond Worms and Speyer; in the North, it went all the way up to the area around Kassel. But it never progressed much further than that. By the late Middle Ages the stretch of land known as Franconia had become very small. Anyone referring to the "Land zu Franken", meant the area between Steigerwald and Spessart, the heart of the Prince Bishopric of Würzburg. It wasn't until 1500 that the Archduchy of Franconia was formed and provided the region with stability and a sense of Franconian identity. It combined the Prince Bishoprics of Bamberg, Würzburg and Eichstatt; the Margraviates of Ansbach and Kulmbach-Bayreuth; the areas around Mergentheim and Ellingen that were under the reign of the Teutonic Knights; the Free Imperial Cities of Nuremberg, Rothenburg, Schweinfurt, Weißenburg and Windsheim; and a long list of other earls and lords that included Henneberg, Hohenlohe, Wertheim, Castell, Rieneck, Schwarzenberg, Schenk von Limpurg, Schenk von Erbach. This Franconia stretched from the Bohemian border to the Odenwald, from Salzungen (which is part of Thuringia today) all the way to Eichstätt.

The Franconian Imperial Circle stretched beyond the region where the Franconian dialect was spoken – to this day, the inhabitants of the Fichtelgebirge speak the Northern Bavarian dialect called *Nordbairisch*. On the other hand, the Saxon duchies south of the Thuringian Forest, where the local people spoke a more Franconian dialect, did not belong to the Franconian Imperial Circle.

Franconia was fragmented. Alongside the earldoms, Free Imperial Cities and prince bishoprics were hundreds of places ruled by various knights. The knights, who belonged to the lower nobility, had been granted freedom from the authority of the local princes in the 16th century. They and their villages were the direct subjects of the Emperor, and not the local rulers.

Characterized by constant conflicts and infighting, Franconia was erased from the map in the early 19th century. After the Kingdom of Prussia annexed the Prince Bishoprics of Ansbach and Bayreuth, in 1792, Bavaria assimilated a large part of Franconia in 1802: first the counties under church administration and most of the Free Imperial Cities, then in 1806 Ansbach, Nuremberg and the many villages belonging to the local gentry; and in 1810 Bayreuth. Bavaria lost the city of Würzburg in 1805, but recovered it in 1814. Other parts of Franconia (the areas around the Jagst and Tauber, or the Odenwald) became part of Hesse, Baden and Württemberg.

At the time, Bavaria's rulers wanted to form a unified state and speaking of "Franconia" was frowned upon. In 1808, Bavaria was divided into administrative regions that, following the French example, were named for rivers. Historical facts played little role in the names chosen.

It wasn't until 1837, when Bavaria was restructured, that the old "tribal" borders were taken into consideration again and the new names reflected the historical past: "Upper Franconia", "Middle Franconia", and "Lower Franconia and Aschaffenburg". This last name was historically accurate because the Lower Main area surrounding of Aschaffenburg had not been considered part of Franconia throughout most of its history.

But through its connection with Lower Franconia, this region became part of Franconia too.

Prof. Dr Günther Dippold, Bezirksheimatpfleger und Cultural Advisor to the county of Upper Franconia and Honorary Professor at the Otto-Friedrich-University in Bamberg

4 3 2 1 | 2017 2016 2015 2014

www.haedecke-verlag.de

Rezepte und Vorwort: Franziska Hanel
Text zu Frankens Historie:
Prof. Dr. Günter Dippold
Übersetzung ins Englische: Lyra Turnbull
Foodfotografie und Styling:
Angela Francisca Endress
Food: Helga Heubner

Bildnachweis:
© Bürgermeister- und Presseamt der Stadt Fürth/Fotograf: Norbert Mittelsdorf (Seite 7, oben rechts); © Congress-Tourismus-Wirtschaft Würzburg/Fotograf: A. Bestle (Seite 6, oben links; Seite 80, 2. von unten; Seite 81, unten links); © Fürstlich Castell'sches Domänenamt (Seite 6, unten; Seite 7, oben Mitte; Seite 11; Seite 80, unten rechts; Seite 81, oben links); © Hädecke Verlag (Seite 81, oben rechts und unten rechts/Angela Francisca Endress; Seite 6, oben rechts; Seite 7, unten links; Seite 10/Chris Meier BFF); © Haus des Gastes, Gößweinstein/Fotograf: David Heßler (Seite 6, Mitte links); © Hemera/Fotograf: AMzPhoto (Seite 80, Mitte rechts); © Stadt Spalt (Seite 6, oben Mitte; Seite 81, oben Mitte); © Touristinformation Muggendorf (Seite 80, oben rechts; Seite 81, Mitte); © restliche Bilder, alle iStock (Seite 6, Mitte rechts/micha_h; Mitte/Valeri Thoermer; Seite 7, oben links/SeanPavonePhoto; Mitte/pilgrimego; unten links/Jchambers; Seite 80, oben links/LianeM; oben Mitte/Typehistorian; Mitte links/Sean Nel; unten links/manfredxy)

Lektorat: Monika Graff
Redaktion: nvsg
Umschlaggestaltung: Julia Graff
Typografie und Satz: ES Typo-Graphic, Ellen Steglich, Stuttgart
Reproduktion: FSM Premedia, Münster
Druck: GCC, Calbe

ISBN 978-3-7750-0662-4

Recipes and preface: Franziska Hanel
Text of Franconia's history:
Prof. Dr. Günter Dippold
English translation: Lyra Turnbull
Food photographs, styling and endpapers:
Angela Francisca Endress

Pictures: © mayor's and pr's office, town of Fürth/photographer: Norbert Mittelsdorf (page 7, first line on the right); © congress tourism commerce, town of Würzburg/photographer: A. Bestle (page 6, first line on the left; page 80, second from below; page 81, last line on the left); © Fürstlich Castell'sches Domänenamt (page 6, last line; page 7, first line in the middle; page 11; page 80, last line on the right; page 81, first line on the left); © Hädecke Verlag (page 81, first line on the right and last line on the right/Angela Francisca Endress; page 6, first line on the right; page 7, last line on the left; page 10/Chris Meier BFF); © visitor's centre, Gößweinstein/photographer: David Heßler (page 6, in the middle on the left); © Hemera/ photographer: AMzPhoto (page 80, in the middle on the right); © town of Spalt (page 6, first line in the middle; page 81, first line in the middle); © Tourist Information Muggendorf (page 80, first line on the right; page 81, in the middle); © for the rest of the pictures, all iStock (page 6, in the middle on the right/micha_h; in the middle/Valeri Thoermer; page 7, first line on the left/SeanPavone Photo; in the middle/pilgrimego; last line on the left/Jchambers; page 80, first line on the left/ LianeM; first line in the middle/Typehistorian; in the middle on the left/Sean Nel; last line on the left/manfredxy)

Editor: Monika Graff
Editorial department: nvsg
Cover design: Julia Graff
Typography and typesetting:
ES Typo-Graphic, Ellen Steglich, Stuttgart
Reproductions: FSM Premedia, Münster
Printing: GCC, Calbe

Printed in Germany 2014

Bildlegenden/Picture captions

Seiten 6–7/pages 6–7

1 Rokoko-Fassade, Falkenhaus Würzburg
2 Spalter Hopfen
3 Reichelshofen (in der Nähe von Rothenburg ob der Tauber, Mittelfranken)
4 Nürnberger Altstadt
5 Portugieser Weinrebe
6 Fürther Rathaus
7 Markt Gößweinstein, Wallfahrtsort mit Basilika (Fränkische Schweiz)
8 Kirschblüte in der Fränkischen Schweiz
9 Altes Bamberger Rathaus
10 Veste Coburg
11 Müller-Thurgau, Rebensorte
12 Morgenstimmung in Castell (Unterfranken)
13 Schloss Johannisburg, Aschaffenburg
14 Bierkultur in Franken

1 Rococo front, Falkenhaus on Market Square, Würzburg
2 Hops from Spalt
3 Reichelshofen (near Rothenburg ob der Tauber, Middle Franconia)
4 Nuremberg, historic district
5 Portugieser grape
6 Fürth, town hall
7 Gößweinstein, place of pilgrimage with basilica (Franconian Switzerland)
8 Cherry blossom, Franconian Switzerland
9 Bamberg, old town hall
10 Coburg Fortress
11 Müller-Thurgau, vine
12 Morgenstimmung in Castell (Lower Franconia)
13 Johannisburg Palace, Aschaffenburg
14 Beer culture in Franconia: "May God preserve, both hops and malt"

Seiten 80–81/pages 80–81

1 Pottenstein (Fränkische Schweiz)
2 Haupteingang des Bamberger Doms
3 Riesenburg bei Doos, Wiesenttal
4 Schlosskeller, Weingut Domäne Castell
5 Hopfenernte beim Hopfengartenfest in Spalt
6 Seßlach (mittelalterliches Städtchen in Oberfranken, Coburger Land)
7/8 Nürnberger Christkindlesmarkt
9 an der Wiesent
10 Würzburger Weinberge mit Blick auf die Festung Marienberg und den Maschikuliturm
11 Forchheim (Oberfranken)
12 Spitzenweinlage Casteller Schlossberg
13 Winterliches Würzburg
14 oberhalb Schloss Geyersberg, Seßlach

1 Pottenstein (Franconian Switzerland)
2 Main Gate, Bamberg Cathedral
3 Riesenburg near Doos, Wiesent Valley
4 Wine cellar, wine-growing estate Castell
5 Hopping at hops festival in Spalt
6 Seßlach (medieval town in Upper Franconia, Coburg land)
7/8 Nuremberg Christmas Market
9 on the river Wiesent
10 Würzburg vineyards, view onto Fortress Marienberg and Maschikuli Tower
11 Forchheim (Upper Franconia)
12 Premium Vineyard Casteller Schlossberg
13 Würzburg in winter
14 above Geyersberg Castle, Seßlach

Danksagung/Acknowledgments

Ein herzliches Dankeschön an alle, die uns bei diesem Buch mit Rat und Tat unterstützt haben! Im Besonderen an: Metzger Marcus Brehm, Seßlach-Dietersdorf; Prof.Dr. Günter Dippold, Historiker, Volkskundler, Honorarprofessor und Bezirksheimatpfleger, Oberfranken; Metzger Sven Fischer, Ahorn- Schafhof; Helga Heubner, Köchin aus Leidenschaft und Foodstilistin, Seßlach-Gemünda; Christine Jaeger vom Gasthhof zum Falken, Mainbernheim; Confiserie Neef, Nürnberg (www.confiserie-neef.de); Stefan Pachsteffl, einer der Seßlacher „Mönche“ (Kommunbrauhaus Seßlach); Heidemarie Roth, Inhaberin der Brotzeitstube mit Biergarten „Schäferstuben“ im Gerätemuseum Coburg-Ahorn (Vorsatz-Fotomotiv); Bäcker und Bäckerin Adolf und Ursula Schoder, Seßlach; Hopfenbotschafterin Elisabeth Stiglmaier, Attenhofen (www.hopfenfuehrung.de); Adrian Vondran, Fischzüchter, Coburg-Seidmannsdorf.

Our sincere thanks to all who have helped produce this book! In particular: butcher, Marcus Brehm, Seßlach-Dietersdorf; Prof.Dr. Günter Dippold, historian, folklorist and Honorary Professor, Upper Franconia; butcher Sven Fischer, Ahorn- Schafhof; Helga Heubner, passionate cook and food stylist, Seßlach-Gemünda; Christine Jaeger from Gasthof zum Falken, Mainbernheim; Confiserie Neef, Nürnberg (www.confiserie-neef.de); Stefan Pachsteffl, one of the Seßlach „monks“ (Kommunbrauhaus Seßlach); Heidemarie Roth, owner of the “Schäferstuben”, a small tavern and beer garden in the Technical Museum (Gerätemuseum), Coburg-Ahorn (endpaper's photograph); bakers, Adolf and Ursula Schoder, Seßlach; hop expert, Elisabeth Stiglmaier, Attenhofen (www.hopfenfuehrung.de – only in German); Adrian Vondran, fish breeder, Coburg-Seidmannsdorf.

Spezialitäten und Genüsse aus Deutschland

Aus Deutschlands Küchen

von Horst Scharfenberg,
775 Seiten,
ISBN 978-3-7750-0415-2.

Quer durch Deutschland, von Schleswig-Holstein bis Bayern, vom Saarland bis Sachsen und Thüringen, werden Originalrezepte aus allen Regionen vorgestellt, sorgfältig recherchiert aus alten Kochbüchern und handschriftlichen Notizen. Eine Fundgrube teilweise fast vergessener Küchenschätze!

Brauereigasthöfe mit Charme
Privatbrauereien
und ihre Lieblingsrezepte

von Chris Meier, 186 Seiten,
227 Farbfotos,
ISBN 978-3-7750-0629-3.

Hopfen und Malz sowie gutes Essen: 29 Adressen von privaten Brauereigasthöfen, die sich durch ihr Bier, ihre Gastlichkeit und einen ganz besonderen Charme auszeichnen. Hier lässt sich vorzüglich essen, trinken und meist auch übernachten. Dazu stellen Bierbrauer, Wirte und Wirtinnen ihre Lieblingsrezepte vor.

HÄDECKE

Weitere Informationen über unsere Kochbücher senden wir Ihnen gerne zu!

Hädecke Verlag GmbH & Co. KG
Postfach 1203
71256 Weil der Stadt/Deutschland

Fax +49(0)7033/1380813
Mail info@haedecke-verlag.de
www.haedecke-verlag.de